Nurturing Mental Wellness

A Guide to Recovery

Lathen Howard

Table of Contents

Chapter 1: Understanding Mental Wellness

Understanding Mental Wellness

In an era where mental health is increasingly recognized as a crucial component of our lives, understanding mental wellness has never been more important. Many people juggle demanding careers, personal relationships, and daily stressors without realizing the toll it takes on their mental state. Just as we strive to maintain physical fitness, nurturing mental wellness is vital for leading a balanced and fulfilling life. By delving into the subtleties of mental well-being, we can uncover practices that not only alleviate psychological distress but also promote overall happiness and resilience.

The modern world's pressures often lead to a neglect of mental health, creating a myriad of both obvious and subtle problems. For instance, consider how chronic stress from tight work deadlines or unresolved personal conflicts can manifest physically as headaches, digestive issues, or even heart disease. Similarly, lack of mental self-care might result in emotional outbursts, insomnia, or feelings of hopelessness. The ripple effects extend further—strained relationships, diminished productivity, and a depreciated sense of self-worth become common.

Therefore, acknowledging and addressing these signs early can prevent them from escalating into more severe conditions such as depression, anxiety, or worse.

In this chapter, we will explore the importance of mental health and its profound impact on overall well-being. We'll discuss the interconnectedness between mental and physical health, revealing how lifestyle choices in diet, exercise, and rest play significant roles. Moreover, we will identify practical strategies for enhancing mental wellness, including recognizing symptoms of mental strain, managing stress effectively, and knowing when to seek professional help. Through a holistic approach that merges scientific insights with actionable advice, this chapter aims to equip you with the knowledge to foster robust mental health, thereby improving your life's quality and joy.

Understanding the Link Between Mental Wellness and Physical Health

Understanding the link between mental wellness and physical health can be a game-changer in your overall well-being. This connection is profound and extensively supported by research from around the world.

Physical and mental health are interconnected, with one influencing the other profoundly. Think of it this way: when your body feels good, so does your mind. Imagine the joy after a brisk walk or the calm after a yoga session. Engaging in activities that promote physical well-being can uplift your mood, reduce anxiety, and help you handle stress more effectively. For example, regular exercise has been shown to improve symptoms of depression and anxiety (Frederick Health, 2021).

Here is what you can do to harness this connection for better health:

- Engage in regular physical activities such as walking, jogging, swimming, or yoga. These activities not only keep your body fit but also release endorphins, the natural mood lifters.

- Avoid prolonged inactivity. Even small bouts of movement throughout the day can add up to significant benefits for both your physical and mental health.

- Find an activity that brings you joy. When you enjoy what you're doing, you're more likely to stick with it.

Proper nutrition, exercise, and adequate rest play crucial roles in maintaining both mental and physical health. It's essential to understand that what you feed your body directly affects your brain's functioning. Eating nutritious meals rich in proteins, essential fats, vitamins, minerals, and complex carbohydrates can prevent mental health conditions like depression and lower your risk of physical ailments like heart disease and type 2 diabetes (Frederick Health, 2021).

To maintain balanced nutrition and support overall well-being:

- Prioritize a diet that includes plenty of fruits, vegetables, lean proteins, and whole grains. These foods provide the necessary nutrients that your brain needs to function optimally.

- Ensure you stay hydrated. Drinking enough water is vital for maintaining cognitive functions and energy levels.

- Limit intake of processed foods and sugars, which can negatively impact your mood and energy.

Exercise goes hand in hand with good nutrition. Regular physical activity is not just about keeping fit; it's about enhancing your mental resilience and reducing the risks of numerous diseases. Studies have found that exercise can significantly improve mental health traits, especially self-concept and body image (Agrawal et al., 2023). Activities like running, cycling, boxing, and yoga can be particularly beneficial. Running can regulate mood, boxing releases endorphins, and yoga helps with relaxation (Frederick Health, 2021).

Recognizing the signs of physical ailments caused by mental stress can prompt individuals to seek support for their overall well-being. It's crucial to pay attention to your body's signals. Stress can manifest in various physical forms - headaches, fatigue, digestive problems, and insomnia. Anxiety might result in stomach issues and restlessness. By being mindful of these symptoms, you can take proactive steps to address them before they escalate.

For instance:

- If you notice persistent headaches or muscle tension, consider if stress might be the underlying cause and take steps to manage it through relaxation techniques or physical activity.

- Fatigue and digestive issues may often indicate that you are not consuming proper nutrients or getting adequate rest. Adjusting your diet and sleep habits can help you feel more energized and less anxious.

Seeking professional help for physical symptoms related to mental health issues can lead to a holistic approach to wellness. Sometimes, self-care measures aren't enough, and professional guidance becomes essential. Seeking help from healthcare providers can offer you comprehensive care tailored to both your mental and physical health needs.

Here's how to approach this:

- If you experience physical symptoms that persist despite efforts to manage them through lifestyle changes, consult a healthcare provider to rule out any serious conditions.

- Don't hesitate to seek mental health support. Professionals like psychologists, therapists, and psychiatrists can provide counseling, medication management, and strategies for coping with stress and anxiety.

- Consider integrative approaches offered by behavioral health services, which may include emergency evaluations, inpatient or partial hospitalization services, and follow-up care tailored to your specific needs (Frederick Health, 2021).

Understanding the importance of caring for both mental and physical health is paramount for overall well-being. Ignoring one aspect can undermine the other, leading to a vicious cycle of deteriorating health. By adopting a holistic view and recognizing the symbiotic relationship between your mind and body, you can navigate life's challenges more resiliently and build a healthier, happier life.

In summary, the interplay between mental and physical health is undeniable. Engagement in regular physical activity, maintaining proper nutrition, recognizing stress-related physical symptoms, and seeking professional help when needed are all crucial steps towards achieving optimal health. By prioritizing both mental and physical well-being, you not only enhance your quality of life but also empower yourself to handle pressures with greater ease and grace. This balanced approach fosters a positive cycle where feeling good physically boosts mental health, and mental well-being encourages physical vitality.

Recognizing Signs of Mental Health Struggles

Recognizing signs of mental health struggles is the first step toward proactive intervention and support. Understanding when someone may be experiencing a mental health issue can mean the difference between them suffering in silence and receiving the help they need. While it might sometimes feel like we are navigating unfamiliar territory, recognizing specific warning signs can provide crucial insights.

One of the most telling indicators of mental health struggles is changes in behavior. You might notice someone who is typically outgoing becoming withdrawn, or someone who is generally easy-going suddenly displaying uncharacteristic anger or hostility. Behavioral changes can also manifest through disruptions in daily routines, such as neglecting responsibilities at home or work, losing interest in activities previously enjoyed, or isolating oneself from friends and family. Mood swings are another red flag—dramatic shifts from happiness to deep sadness, excessive irritability, or unexplained bouts of crying can all signal underlying issues. Additionally, difficulties in daily functioning, such as trouble concentrating, memory lapses, or an inability to perform everyday tasks, can indicate that something more serious may be at play (The Jed Foundation, n.d.).

Here is what you can do to identify common signs of mental health struggles:

- Pay attention to significant changes in someone's behavior. This could include sudden withdrawal from social activities, neglect of personal hygiene, or loss of interest in hobbies.

- Observe mood swings and emotional extremes. Notice if someone is oscillating between highs and lows much more frequently than usual.

- Look for signs of difficulty in managing daily tasks. This might involve consistent tardiness, inability to focus on work, or forgetfulness about routine responsibilities.

- Be mindful of physical symptoms related to mental distress, such as unexplained fatigue, insomnia, or drastic changes in appetite.

- Trust your instincts. If you sense that something is off with a friend or loved one, it's worth exploring these feelings further.

Understanding that early recognition of mental health struggles can lead to timely intervention is crucial. Early intervention has been shown to significantly mitigate the severity of mental health conditions, making them easier to manage over time. Just as with physical illnesses, addressing mental health concerns promptly can prevent them from escalating into more serious issues. This knowledge emphasizes the need for awareness and vigilance in identifying potential problems before they become overwhelming (Psychiatry.org, n.d.).

Educating ourselves and others about the stigma surrounding mental health struggles is equally important. Many people suffer in silence because they fear being judged or misunderstood. Stigma can prevent individuals from seeking the help they desperately need, exacerbating their condition. By fostering an understanding that mental health struggles are not a sign of weakness but rather a genuine medical concern, we can encourage more people to come forward and seek treatment without shame or fear. Changing our societal attitudes towards mental health begins with each of us accepting that these issues are a normal part of the human experience, deserving of compassion and support (Mental Health America, n.d.).

Encouraging open communication about mental health concerns is perhaps one of the most powerful tools we have in breaking the cycle of silence and stigma. Talking openly about mental health in our circles can foster a supportive environment where individuals feel safe to express their struggles. It's beneficial to create spaces where conversations around mental health are normalized, whether at home, in schools, or workplaces. By doing so, we can help those who might be suffering feel less isolated and more inclined to reach out for help.

To promote open dialogue, consider the following steps:

- Initiate conversations about mental health regularly, not just during crises. This helps normalize the topic and makes it easier for people to share their experiences.

- Share your own experiences with mental health struggles, if comfortable. Personal stories can dispel myths and show others that they are not alone.

- Encourage others to share their feelings without judgment. Create a non-threatening environment by actively listening and showing empathy.

- Use inclusive and non-stigmatizing language when discussing mental health. Avoid phrases that could inadvertently shame or belittle someone's experience.

- Provide resources and information about where to find professional help. Make it clear that seeking help is a positive and courageous step.

Empowering individuals to recognize and address mental health struggles proactively is essential. When people feel equipped to identify early warning signs in themselves or others, they can take timely actions that might include seeking therapy, practicing self-care techniques, or simply talking to a trusted person about their feelings. Understanding that mental health is just as vital as physical health can inspire a more preventative approach, reducing the overall impact on an individual's life.

Mental health struggles affect all aspects of well-being, including our physical health, relationships, and productivity. By learning to recognize these struggles early, encouraging open communication, and debunking the stigma associated with them, we pave the way for healthier, more supportive communities. We all have a role to play in promoting mental health awareness and support, ensuring that no one has to face these challenges alone.

Remember, the journey to better mental health starts with understanding and taking small, meaningful steps. Whether it's paying closer attention to behavioral changes, having an honest conversation with a friend, or advocating for mental health education in your community, each action contributes to a larger movement toward a society that values and protects the mental well-being of its members.

Understanding the Role of Stress in Mental Well-being

Stress can impact mental health by triggering anxiety, depression, and other emotional challenges. Whether it's the nagging worry about meeting a deadline, the overwhelming burden of financial worries, or the quiet yet persistent dread of unknown future events, stress is an inescapable part of our modern lives. Yet, while some level of stress can indeed spur us into action—boosting performance and heightening our senses—prolonged exposure to stress can be decidedly harmful.

When stress becomes chronic, it starts to take a toll on both our minds and bodies. Studies have shown that ongoing stress can lead to a multitude of mental health issues, such as anxiety and depression (How stress affects your health, n.d.). This happens because chronic stress results in the constant release of stress hormones like adrenaline and cortisol, which over time can alter brain function, affect immune responses, and even accelerate aging processes. So, it's crucial to recognize when stress has crossed from being a temporary motivator to becoming a chronic problem that undermines well-being.

Recognizing this, we then turn to stress management techniques as practical interventions. Managing stress can be approached from several angles, and incorporating multiple strategies often yields the best results. Here are some effective techniques you can try to support mental well-being:

- **Mindfulness:** One of the most powerful tools for managing stress is mindfulness. Being present and fully engaged with the current moment can reduce anxiety about past or future events. You can start with simple practices like deep breathing, a short meditation session, or merely paying attention to your surroundings without judgment.

- **Relaxation Exercises:** Engaging in activities that relax the body and mind, such as yoga, progressive muscle relaxation, and guided imagery, can lower the physiological response to stress. Even small acts, like listening to calming music or taking a hot bath, can make a big difference.

- **Time Management:** Sometimes, stress stems from feeling overwhelmed by impending tasks. Effective time management involves prioritizing tasks, breaking them down into manageable steps, and giving yourself permission to say no when necessary. Utilizing planners or digital tools can help you keep track and reduce that frazzled feeling.

Healthy stress, known as "eustress," fuels our creativity, productivity, and overall sense of accomplishment. It's the type of stress that gets you excited before a big project or motivates you to improve your skills. In contrast, chronic stress is relentless and wears you down physically and mentally. Understanding this difference is vital for recognizing when to take action.

Developing coping strategies to navigate stressors is another critical aspect of maintaining mental well-being. Building resilience doesn't mean avoiding stress altogether but rather learning how to handle it effectively when it arises. Here's what you can do:

- Identify your stress triggers. Awareness is the first step in managing stress. Keep a journal to track situations that cause stress and your responses to them.

- Build a support network. Having friends, family, or colleagues you can talk to helps buffer against stress. Opening up about your feelings with someone you trust can provide emotional support and alternative perspectives.

- Maintain a healthy lifestyle. Regular physical activity, balanced nutrition, and sufficient sleep can bolster your resilience. Exercise, in particular, has been shown to reduce levels of stress hormones while stimulating the production of endorphins, which can improve mood.

- Practice self-care rituals. Taking regular breaks, engaging in hobbies, or treating yourself kindly can recharge your batteries. Make sure you set aside time each day for activities that bring you joy and relaxation.

- Seek professional help if needed. Sometimes, the best way to manage overwhelming stress is through professional help. Therapists and counselors can assist in developing personalized strategies to cope with stress and its impacts effectively.

Learning to manage stress effectively is not just optional; it's essential for improved mental well-being. Chronic stress doesn't just exist in the mind; it reverberates through every facet of your physical health, relationships, and daily life. By implementing these stress management techniques and coping strategies, you can reclaim a sense of control and build a more resilient mindset.

It's worth noting that managing stress is an ongoing process rather than a one-time fix. It requires practice, patience, and persistence. The journey towards effective stress management is deeply personal, reflecting your unique experiences, preferences, and circumstances. Remember to be kind to yourself throughout this journey. Each small step you take toward managing stress better is a victory worth celebrating, contributing to a healthier, happier you.

The impact of stress can be profound, but with the right tools and approaches, it's possible to mitigate its negative effects and significantly improve your overall quality of life. Balancing day-to-day pressures with mindful practices and supportive habits can pave the way for enduring mental wellness and a richer, more fulfilling existence.

Exploring the Benefits of Seeking Professional Help

Professional help, such as therapy or counseling, can be transformative for mental health. Imagine trying to fix a complex piece of machinery without the proper tools—it's nearly impossible and often leads to more harm than good. Similarly, addressing mental health concerns without the right support can be overwhelming. Trained professionals offer not just an empathetic ear but practical tools that empower individuals to manage their mental health more effectively.

Here is what you can do in order to achieve this:

- Start by acknowledging that seeking help is a sign of strength. It's the first step towards gaining control over your mental well-being.

- Look for local therapists or counselors through credible sources. Your primary care doctor can provide recommendations, or you can search online directories accredited by professional bodies.

- Don't be afraid to ask questions. Inquire about a professional's experience with issues similar to yours, their approach to treatment, and whether they accept your insurance.

- Be persistent. If the first therapist isn't the right fit, it's okay to try another until you find someone with whom you feel comfortable.

Engaging in therapy or counseling equips you with coping mechanisms tailored to your specific needs, from relaxation techniques to stress management strategies. According to High Country Behavioral Health (2023), developing these skills can significantly enhance your ability to navigate life's challenges, leading to improved relationships and increased self-esteem. It's like learning a new language; initially, it feels foreign, but with time, it becomes second nature, enriching your life in countless ways.

Highlighting the importance of trained professionals in diagnosing and treating mental health issues cannot be overstated. While it might be tempting to lean on friends or self-help books, professionals bring a depth of expertise that is indispensable. They have undergone rigorous training to understand the nuances of various mental health conditions and how to address them effectively. Think of it this way: while friends and family provide essential emotional support, they don't have the clinical knowledge to diagnose or treat mental health disorders properly.

Research underscores that most people who seek professional help experience significant improvements. Mental Health America (n.d.) notes that over 80% of individuals treated for depression report feeling better, and treatments for panic disorders boast success rates up to 90%. These figures highlight the tangible benefits of professional intervention, offering hope and evidence that recovery is possible with the right help.

Yet, despite these advantages, many hesitate to seek professional aid due to stigma, misconceptions, or fears. Overcoming these barriers is crucial for prioritizing mental well-being. Stigma, in particular, deters many from taking that vital first step towards getting help. According to King et al. (2014), a significant barrier students face is the embarrassment and denial surrounding mental health issues. This social stigma fosters a harmful cycle where individuals avoid seeking help, worsening their conditions over time.

To break this cycle:

- Normalize conversations around mental health. Share your experiences openly if you're comfortable, as this encourages others to speak up about their struggles.

- Educate yourself and others about mental health. Understanding that mental health issues are common and treatable reduces the fear and shame associated with them.

- Seek communities that foster open discussions about mental health, either online or in-person. These spaces provide support and reassurance that you're not alone.

- Remember that seeking help is a proactive step towards better health, comparable to seeing a doctor for a physical ailment. It's an act of self-care, not a sign of weakness.

By addressing these barriers head-on, you not only improve your own mental health but also pave the way for others to seek the help they need. The impact of reducing stigma can ripple through communities, making it easier for everyone to prioritize their mental well-being without fear of judgment.

Encouraging a collaborative approach between individuals and mental health professionals is another essential factor for effective mental health treatment. Recovery is not a one-size-fits-all process. Just as a tailor customizes clothing to fit an individual's unique measurements, mental health treatments should be tailored to fit the individual's needs. Collaboration ensures that both the patient and the professional are actively involved in the treatment process, fostering a sense of ownership and commitment.

Here is what you can do to foster this collaborative approach:

- Communicate openly with your therapist. Share your goals and concerns so they can tailor their approach to suit your needs.

- Actively participate in your treatment plan. Engage in suggested activities and practice coping strategies outside of therapy sessions.

- Provide feedback to your therapist. If something isn't working, let them know so adjustments can be made.

- Be patient and persistent. Understand that recovery takes time and effort from both sides.

This joint effort creates a supportive environment where treatment can be most effective. As Mental Health America (n.d.) highlights, talking about personal issues may be tough initially, but developing coping skills and building stronger relationships result in long-term benefits. When both parties are committed to the process, the journey toward recovery is smoother and more productive.

In conclusion, understanding the value of professional support in enhancing mental wellness is imperative. It's about equipping oneself with the right tools, breaking down the barriers that deter people from seeking help, and fostering a partnership with professionals for better outcomes. Seeking help when needed is not only a wise decision but a courageous one. It's a testament to one's commitment to improving their well-being and living a fulfilling life. By prioritizing mental health and encouraging others to do the same, we contribute to a society where mental wellness is held in the same regard as physical health, ultimately benefiting us all.

Holistic Approaches to Mental and Physical Well-being

Understanding the profound connection between mental wellness and physical health is a crucial aspect of overall well-being. Throughout this chapter, we have explored how engaging in regular physical activities, maintaining proper nutrition, and recognizing stress-related physical symptoms can significantly improve mental health. We've also discussed how these practices help in reducing anxiety, uplifting mood, and better managing everyday stress.

We began by examining the symbiotic relationship between physical and mental health, illustrating how one influences the other deeply. When our body feels good, our mind follows suit, and vice versa. By prioritizing activities that bring joy and relaxation, such as walking or yoga, and paying attention to balanced nutrition, individuals can create a foundation for both mental and physical vitality.

Moreover, we highlighted the importance of recognizing early signs of distress, whether they manifest as physical symptoms like headaches and fatigue or behavioral changes such as withdrawal from social interactions. Understanding these signals allows for timely intervention, potentially preventing more severe health issues down the line.

Considering the holistic view of health, it's essential to mention that ignoring either mental or physical well-being can set off a detrimental cycle where one negatively impacts the other. This underscores the need for a balanced approach, incorporating self-care practices and professional support when necessary. Addressing mental health struggles openly and without stigma can pave the way for more supportive communities and better individual outcomes.

As we move forward, remember that adopting a proactive stance toward your health empowers you to handle life's pressures with greater ease. The interplay between physical activities, nutrition, and mental well-being forms a positive feedback loop, enhancing quality of life and fostering resilience against future challenges.

In conclusion, nurturing both your mind and body is vital for achieving optimal health. By integrating physical well-being practices into your routine, staying mindful of nutritional choices, and seeking professional guidance when needed, you establish a robust foundation for enduring happiness and strength. Reflect on how you can implement these strategies in your daily life, and consider the broader impact on your journey towards a healthier, more fulfilling existence.

References

American Psychiatric Association. (n.d.). *Warning Signs of Mental Illness* . Retrieved from https://www.psychiatry.org/patients-families/warning-signs-of-mental-illness

Ohrnberger, J., Fichera, E., & Sutton, M. (2017). *The relationship between physical and mental health: A mediation analysis* . Social Science & Medicine (1982) , 195, 10.1016/j.socscimed.2017.11.008. https://doi.org/10.1016/j.socscimed.2017.11.008

JED Foundation. (2023). *Mental Health Warning Signs and When to Ask for Help* . The Jed Foundation. Retrieved from https://jedfoundation.org/resource/mental-health-warning-signs-and-when-to-ask-for-help/

Mental Health America. (n.d.). *Mental Illness and the Family: Recognizing Warning Signs and How to Cope* . Retrieved from https://www.mhanational.org/recognizing-warning-signs

Schneiderman, N., Ironson, G., & Siegel, S. D. (2005). *STRESS AND HEALTH: Psychological, Behavioral, and Biological Determinants* . *Annual Review of Clinical Psychology* , 1, 607. https://doi.org/10.1146/annurev.clinpsy.1.102803.144141

Yaribeygi, H., Panahi, Y., Sahraei, H., Johnston, T. P., & Sahebkar, A. (2017). *The impact of stress on body function: A review* . *EXCLI Journal* , 16(1057), 10.17179/excli2017-480. https://doi.org/10.17179/excli2017-480

American Psychological Association. (n.d.). *How stress affects your health* . https://www.apa.org/topics/stress/health

Mahindru, A., Patil, P., & Agrawal, V. (2023). *Role of physical activity on mental health and well-being: A review* . *Cureus* , 15(1), Article 10.7759/cureus. 33475. https://doi.org/10.7759/cureus.33475

Vidourek, R. A., King, K. A., Nabors, L. A., & Merianos, A. L. (2014). *Students' benefits and barriers to mental health help-seeking* . *Health Psychology and Behavioral Medicine* , 1(2), 1009. https://doi.org/10.1080/21642850.2014.963586

Mental Health America. (n.d.). *Get Professional Help If You Need It* . Retrieved from https:// mhanational.org/get-professional-help-if-you-need-it

Frederick Health. (2021). *The connection between mental and physical health* . Frederick Health. Retrieved from https://www.frederickhealth.org/ news/2021/october/the-connection-between-mental-and-physical-healt/

High Country Behavioral Health. (2023). *Benefits to seeking professional help for your mental health concerns* . Retrieved from https://www.hcbh.org/ blog/posts/2023/may/benefits-to-seeking-professional-help-for-your-mental-health-concerns/

Chapter 2: Healing From Past Trauma

Healing from Past Trauma

Trauma is like an invisible wound, often buried deep within our minds and hearts, yet its effects can be as palpable as physical scars. Many of us carry these unseen burdens from past experiences, struggling to navigate their lingering impact on our daily lives. Imagine your mind as a garden where trauma plants seeds of doubt, fear, and anxiety that grow into thorny barriers obstructing your path to peace and fulfillment. Understanding and addressing these hidden injuries is pivotal in reclaiming control over our mental and emotional well-being.

Consider Jane, who, despite her professional success and loving family, finds herself gripped by intense anxiety during social gatherings. This paralyzing fear traces back to relentless bullying in her school years, which eroded her self-esteem and planted mistrust in human interactions. Or think about Mark, whose struggle with chronic pain and health issues ties back to the traumatic car accident he survived in his youth. These instances highlight how past traumas can shape our present behavior, emotions, and even health. Recognizing this connection is essential for taking the first steps toward healing. It allows us to see the sources of our distress not as random chaos but as pieces of a puzzle we can begin to solve.

In the following chapter, we will explore various ways to identify and understand the roots of our trauma. By delving into specific examples and providing practical tools such as journaling and therapeutic practices, we aim to illuminate the path to healing. You'll learn about the importance of creating safe spaces for self-reflection, seeking professional help, and fostering supportive environments. Each section is designed to empower you with knowledge and strategies to gradually dismantle the barriers trauma has erected, paving the way for inner peace and resilience.

Identifying and Understanding Sources of Trauma

Recognizing past traumatic events can provide insight into current struggles and emotional reactions. Often, the experiences we've had shape not only our behaviors but also our perceptions of the world around us. When we endure trauma, especially in our formative years, it can cast a long shadow over our lives, influencing how we react to stress, build relationships, and handle adversity.

Take, for example, childhood trauma. According to the Adverse Childhood Experiences (ACE) Study, nearly 64% of participants reported experiencing at least one traumatic event during their childhood, with 69% of those reporting two or more incidents (Peterson, 2018). The study found that these early traumas correlated with chronic illnesses such as heart disease and cancer, high-risk behaviors, and even early death. This research suggests that recognizing these traumas can help us understand why certain situations trigger intense emotions or particular behaviors in us today. Imagine you find yourself overly anxious in social settings. Reflecting back, you might realize that being bullied in school or having inconsistent caregivers made you wary and hypervigilant, always on guard for potential threats. This kind of self-awareness is a critical first step toward healing.

Journaling about past traumas can aid in processing and acknowledging difficult emotions. Writing is a powerful tool for self-discovery and emotional release. While it might seem daunting to confront painful memories, putting them down on paper can be incredibly liberating.

To start, set aside some quiet time each day for journaling. Create a safe space—perhaps in a cozy corner of your home where you feel secure. Begin by writing freely without worrying about grammar or structure; just let your thoughts flow. You may choose to write about specific events, how they made you feel then, and how they affect you now. Additionally, consider reflecting on the patterns you notice in your emotional reactions. Do certain triggers take you back to your trauma? How do they manifest in your body and mind? This practice helps in making connections between past events and present feelings, thereby enabling you to address these issues more constructively.

Seeking therapy or counseling can assist in addressing and working through past traumas. Professional guidance offers an invaluable support system as you navigate the complexities of your experiences and emotions. Therapists are trained to provide a non-judgmental space where you can explore your feelings openly and safely.

Here is what you can do in order to achieve the goal:

- Seek recommendations from trusted sources to find a therapist who specializes in trauma.

- Initiate contact and schedule a consultation to discuss your history and goals.

- Be open and honest during sessions; remember, there's no shame in needing support.

- Utilize tools like Cognitive Behavioral Therapy (CBT) or Eye Movement Desensitization and Reprocessing (EMDR), which have shown efficacy in treating trauma (Kleber, 2019).

Therapy sessions can help you develop coping strategies, reframe negative thought patterns, and gradually desensitize your responses to trauma reminders. Over time, this can lead to significant improvements in mental health and overall well-being.

Creating a safe space for self-reflection can help individuals explore the root causes of their trauma. Just as physical safety is essential for survival, emotional safety is crucial for healing. Your environment can greatly influence your ability to reflect and process your feelings.

Here is what you can do in order to achieve the goal:

- Identify a peaceful location where you feel comfortable and undisturbed—this could be a room at home, a favorite park, or even a quiet café.

- Surround yourself with comforting items—soft lighting, soothing music, or meaningful objects.

- Practice mindfulness or meditation to center yourself; focus on your breath and allow your thoughts to settle.

- Start small by reflecting on less intense memories before tackling more challenging experiences.

By creating a sanctuary for reflection, you're fostering an environment that supports introspection and healing. It's a place where you can be vulnerable without fear, enabling you to dig deep into your past and understand its impact on your present.

Healing from past trauma and achieving inner peace is not a linear journey. It involves recognizing and understanding your experiences, expressing and processing emotions through journaling, seeking professional help when necessary, and creating safe environments for self-reflection. Each step is integral to embracing a fuller, healthier life where your well-being takes precedence over external pressures or past pain.

Remember, it's okay to seek help. It's okay to take your time. Most importantly, it's okay to prioritize your own healing. In doing so, you'll not only become more attuned to your own needs but also better equipped to navigate the challenges that life throws your way. Healing allows you to reclaim control over your story and move forward with resilience and hope.

Coping Mechanisms and Strategies

Practicing mindfulness techniques can help individuals stay present and manage distressing thoughts related to trauma. At its core, mindfulness involves paying attention to your current experience without judgment. This simple yet powerful approach allows you to observe your thoughts and feelings from a distance rather than becoming overwhelmed by them.

Here is what you can do in order to achieve the goal:

- Find a quiet space where you won't be disturbed.

- Sit comfortably and close your eyes if it feels right.

- Focus on your breath, noticing each inhale and exhale.

- When distressing thoughts arise, acknowledge them without judging yourself. Gently bring your focus back to your breath.

- Practice this regularly, starting with just a few minutes a day and gradually increasing the time as you feel more comfortable.

Research shows that mindfulness practices can significantly reduce symptoms of PTSD and anxiety (Director, 2019). By cultivating an awareness of the present moment, you can create a mental space that is less dominated by past traumas. Think of it as training your mind to be more resilient, providing yourself with a sanctuary amid the chaos.

Engaging in creative outlets such as art or music can offer a therapeutic way to express and release emotions. Creativity taps into parts of the brain that are often dormant when we are stressed or traumatized. It allows for a form of expression that words might struggle to convey. Painting, drawing, writing music, or even listening to music can become safe spaces for emotional release.

Here is what you can do in order to achieve the goal:

- Choose a medium that appeals to you: painting, drawing, playing an instrument, singing, etc.

- Set aside specific times during your week to engage in these activities.

- Allow yourself to create freely without worrying about the outcome. The process itself is the healing aspect.

- Consider joining a community class or group where you can share your work and experiences with others.

These outlets not only provide a break from intrusive thoughts but also produce tangible results—pieces of art or music that reflect your journey. Many find that these activities help externalize internal turmoil, making it easier to confront and process. Studies show that creative expression can improve mood, reduce stress, and enhance overall well-being (How to cope with traumatic stress, n.d.).

Participating in physical activities like yoga or running can aid in releasing pent-up tension and stress from past traumas. Physical movement is crucial because trauma often manifests in the body. When you're physically active, your body releases endorphins, which are natural mood lifters.

Here is what you can do in order to achieve the goal:

- Start with gentle exercises if you're new to physical activity. Yoga is an excellent option as it combines physical movement with mindful breathing.

- Gradually incorporate more intensive workouts like running or weightlifting as your stamina builds.

- Set realistic goals and celebrate small milestones to keep yourself motivated.

- Try to exercise outdoors, when possible, as fresh air and nature have their own calming effects.

Yoga, in particular, has been lauded for its dual benefits of physical exercise and meditative focus. It encourages deep breathing, stretching, and body awareness—all beneficial for releasing trauma held in the body (Discusses active ways to cope with traumatic stress, with tips for coping with specific PTSD symptoms., 2007).

Connecting with a support group or community of individuals who have experienced similar traumas can offer validation and understanding. Knowing that you are not alone in your experiences is profoundly comforting. Support groups provide a space where you can share your story, hear others' journeys, and find mutual encouragement.

Here is what you can do in order to achieve the goal:

- Look for local or online support groups specialized in trauma or PTSD.

- Attend a few meetings to see if the group dynamic suits you.

- Be open about your experiences but also give yourself permission to pass if you don't feel ready to share.

- Consider one-on-one interactions within the group to build stronger, more personal connections.

In these settings, the collective wisdom and shared empathy can be incredibly healing. You may discover that others have faced similar challenges and developed strategies that could work for you, too. This communal experience helps dismantle feelings of isolation and fosters a sense of belonging, which is crucial for emotional recovery.

Healing from past traumas is undeniably challenging, but these methods offer multiple avenues for relief and empowerment. By integrating mindfulness, creative expression, physical activity, and community support into your life, you can create a holistic strategy for overcoming trauma. Each of these techniques not only addresses different facets of your being but also reinforces your inherent strength and resilience. Remember, this journey is unique to you, and it's okay to take it one step at a time.

Self-Reflection and Acceptance

Embracing vulnerability and acknowledging past traumas without judgment can foster self-acceptance and healing. Each of us carries a unique set of scars and stories that shape who we are today. These experiences, while painful, have contributed to our growth and resilience. By allowing ourselves to confront these past hurts openly and honestly, we begin the journey toward self-reflection and acceptance. It's important to understand that vulnerability is not a sign of weakness; rather, it is a profound demonstration of strength and courage.

Think about those moments when you've shared a deeply personal story with a trusted friend or therapist. The act of verbalizing your pain helps lessen its hold on you. When you acknowledge your traumas without judgment, you're giving yourself permission to feel and process emotions that may have been suppressed for too long. This acknowledgment can serve as a release valve, easing the pressure and providing a sense of relief and clarity.

Practicing forgiveness, both towards oneself and others involved in past traumas, can release emotional burdens and promote inner peace. Forgiveness is a powerful tool in healing because it allows us to let go of resentment and anger, emotions that can weigh heavily on our mental and physical well-being. Here is what you can do in order to achieve this goal:

- Reflect on the reasons why forgiveness is difficult for you. Understanding the barriers can help you approach them more effectively.

- Recognize that forgiveness does not mean excusing or condoning harmful behavior. It's about freeing yourself from the grip of negative emotions.

- Write a letter to yourself or the person involved, expressing your feelings and intentions of forgiveness. You don't have to send it, but the act of writing can be therapeutic.

- Use meditation or mindfulness practices to focus on letting go of grudges and embracing compassion for yourself and others.

- Seek professional guidance if needed. Sometimes, a counselor or therapist can provide strategies and support to help facilitate the process of forgiveness.

Cultivating a growth mindset that views challenges as opportunities for learning and personal development can empower individuals to overcome past traumas. Embracing a growth mindset means believing that abilities and intelligence can be developed through dedication, effort, and persistence. This perspective shifts the focus from "Why did this happen to me?" to "What can I learn from this experience?"

For instance, consider how individuals often gain new skills, resilience, and perspectives after facing adversity. Adopting this mindset helps transform traumatic experiences into steppingstones for personal growth. It encourages individuals to see their struggles as catalysts for change rather than insurmountable obstacles. Whenever you face a challenge, remind yourself that every difficulty carries the potential for valuable lessons and growth.

Engaging in self-care practices like meditation or relaxation exercises can promote emotional regulation and resilience. Self-care goes beyond mere indulgence; it's about nurturing your mind, body, and soul. Engaging in regular self-care routines creates a foundation of stability and well-being that can help buffer the impacts of stress and trauma. Here's a guideline to embed self-care into your daily life:

- Start with small daily rituals like setting aside a few minutes each morning for deep breathing exercises.

- Incorporate physical activities such as yoga or walking, which are excellent for both mental and physical health.

- Practice mindfulness by being present in each moment. Techniques such as mindful eating or even a simple mindfulness meditation can ground you.

- Schedule time for hobbies or activities that bring you joy and relaxation, whether it's reading, gardening, or playing an instrument.

- Ensure you get enough rest. Establish a bedtime routine that promotes good sleep hygiene and helps you wind down at night.

- Stay connected with loved ones. Social support is crucial for resilience, so make regular efforts to communicate and spend time with friends and family.

Navigating the journey of healing from past experiences to achieve inner peace involves a combination of self-reflection, acceptance, and ongoing growth. By embracing vulnerability, practicing forgiveness, cultivating a growth mindset, and engaging in self-care, we build resilience and move toward a state of inner peace. Remember, this journey is uniquely yours, shaped by your experiences and sustained by your efforts to heal and grow.

Building a Supportive Environment

Surrounding oneself with positive and understanding individuals can provide a sense of safety and encouragement in the healing process. Imagine wrapping yourself in a warm blanket on a cold winter's night—that's what it's like to be surrounded by people who genuinely care for your well-being. The support from friends, family, or community members acts as a cushion that softens the blows of past traumas. These individuals don't have to be perfect; they just need to be there, offering an ear, a shoulder, and sometimes just their presence.

When it comes to emotional well-being, establishing boundaries is essential. Think of boundaries as invisible fences that protect our inner peace. Surrounding yourself with supportive individuals is crucial, but equally important is keeping a healthy distance from those who may trigger or exacerbate trauma-related symptoms. Here is what you can do to maintain these boundaries:

- First, recognize who in your life causes you to feel stressed, anxious, or depressed.

- Second, communicate your needs clearly and assertively without feeling guilty.

- Third, limit or avoid interactions with these individuals, especially during times when you are emotionally vulnerable.

- Finally, evaluate and adjust these boundaries as needed, ensuring they serve your mental health effectively.

Remember, setting boundaries is not about erecting walls to isolate yourself, but about creating safe spaces where you can heal and thrive.

Building a self-care routine that prioritizes one's mental health needs is another cornerstone for ongoing healing from past traumas. Self-care isn't just about lighting candles and taking baths—though those can be nice—it's about crafting a daily practice that nurtures your mind and soul. To foster this routine:

- Start by identifying activities that bring you joy and peace. This could be anything from reading a book to gardening or painting.

- Make time each day, even if only for a few minutes, to engage in these activities without distractions.

- Practice mindfulness or meditation to stay grounded and aware of your emotions.

- Ensure you get adequate rest, nutrition, and exercise, as these physical necessities greatly influence mental health.

In essence, self-care routines should fit seamlessly into your lifestyle, gradually becoming habits that bolster your resilience against stress and trauma.

Seeking professional help from therapists or support groups offers another layer of guidance and validation in navigating the complexities of past traumas. Professional therapists are trained to understand the intricacies of trauma and can offer strategies tailored specifically to your experiences. Support groups, on the other hand, provide a communal environment where shared stories and collective wisdom can foster a sense of belonging and hope. Here are steps to effectively utilize professional help:

- Research and find a licensed therapist with experience in trauma. Personal recommendations, online reviews, or directories can be helpful starting points.

- Schedule a consultation session to gauge comfort levels and discuss treatment methods.

- Be open and honest in your sessions; healing requires vulnerability and trust.

- Supplement therapy with support group meetings. Sharing your journey with others facing similar challenges can be incredibly empowering.

It's vital to remember that seeking help is not a sign of weakness but a courageous step towards recovery. The National Institute of Mental Health (NIMH) highlights the importance of professional intervention for those whose trauma symptoms persist and interfere with daily life (National Institute of Mental Health (NIMH), n.d.).

Navigating the journey of healing from past experiences to achieve inner peace is multifaceted, requiring openness, patience, and continual effort. It begins with the simple yet profound act of surrounding oneself with positive influences. Creating a protective, nurturing environment through careful boundary-setting helps mitigate the impact of negative triggers. Incorporating a robust self-care routine aligns daily actions with mental health priorities, cultivating long-term resilience. Lastly, seeking professional guidance ensures specialized support tailored to individual needs, facilitating deeper, sustained healing.

And as we embark on this journey, we must remind ourselves that healing is not linear. There will be days filled with progress and days that feel like setbacks. Both are part of the process. Each step, no matter how small, brings us closer to a place of inner calm and strength. In this collective effort of personal responsibility and social support, we find the balance that enables true healing, bearing witness to our own incredible capacity for growth and renewal.

Embracing the Path to Inner Peace

In understanding the profound journey of healing from past traumas, we have discussed recognizing and comprehending sources of trauma, such as those illuminated by the Adverse Childhood Experiences (ACE) Study. The impact of these early experiences extends far into adulthood, affecting our emotional responses, relationships, and overall health. Acknowledging these past events becomes a pivotal step in making sense of current struggles and initiating the healing process.

Reflecting back on the journaling practice, we've seen how this reflective tool can help untangle complex emotions tied to traumatic experiences. It allows for self-discovery and emotional release, offering a structured method to navigate the labyrinth of painful memories. Similarly, creating safe environments for reflection and seeking professional therapeutic support are critical acts of self-care that foster emotional safety and growth.

As you embark on this journey, it's essential to remember that healing is not a linear path but a series of steps forward and sometimes backward. This reality might be daunting for some, but it's crucial to understand that setbacks are part of the process. They do not negate progress but rather offer opportunities for deeper understanding and resilience-building.

The wider consequences of embracing such practices ripple beyond individual transformation. As more people engage in their own healing, society collectively becomes more empathetic and supportive. Personal well-being bolsters communal strength, leading to healthier relationships and communities.

Ultimately, the journey towards inner peace through healing from past traumas is deeply personal yet universally impactful. Each step you take—whether through self-reflection, professional therapy, or cultivating supportive environments—is a testament to your resilience and capacity for growth. Keep in mind that while the path may be challenging, it also holds immense potential for renewal and empowerment.

Remember, healing is a journey, not a destination. With each moment of mindfulness, self-care, and reflection, you are crafting a life marked by greater understanding, compassion, and peace. Embrace the process, stay patient with yourself, and trust in your ability to heal and thrive.

References

Nugent, N. R., Sumner, J. A., & Amstadter, A. B. (2014). *Resilience after trauma: from surviving to thriving* . *European Journal of Psychotraumatology* , 5(10), 1-12. https://doi.org/10.3402/ejpt.v5.25339

Havertz, S. (2019). *5 Healthy Coping Strategies For Trauma* . *Highland Springs* . Retrieved from https://highlandspringsclinic.org/5-healthy-coping-strategies-after-a-traumatic-event/

American Psychological Association (n.d.). *Building your resilience* . Retrieved from https://www.apa.org/topics/resilience/building-your-resilience

HelpGuide.org. (n.d.). *How to Cope with Traumatic Events - HelpGuide.org* . Retrieved from https://www.helpguide.org/articles/ptsd-trauma/traumatic-stress.htm

Kleber, R. J. (2019). *Trauma and public mental health: A focused review* . *Frontiers in Psychiatry* , 10. https://doi.org/10.3389/fpsyt.2019.00451

American Psychological Association. (n.d.). *How to cope with traumatic stress* . Retrieved from https://www.apa.org/topics/trauma/stress

Substance Abuse and Mental Health Services Administration. (2014). *Understanding the Impact of Trauma* . *Trauma-Informed Care in Behavioral Health Services* . Retrieved from https://www.ncbi.nlm.nih.gov/books/NBK207191/

United States Department of Veterans Affairs (2007). *Discusses active ways to cope with traumatic stress with tips for coping with specific PTSD symptoms. PTSD: National Center for PTSD* . https://www.ptsd.va.gov/gethelp/coping_stress_reactions.asp

National Institute of Mental Health. (n.d.). *Coping With Traumatic Events* . https://www.nimh.nih.gov/health/topics/coping-with-traumatic-events

National Child Traumatic Stress Network. (2018). *Effects* . Retrieved from https://www.nctsn.org/what-is-child-trauma/trauma-types/complex-trauma/effects

HelpGuide.org. (n.d.). *Coping with emotional and psychological trauma* . Retrieved from https://www.helpguide.org/articles/ptsd-trauma/coping-with-emotional-and-psychological-trauma.htm

Mayo Clinic. (2023). *Resilience: Build skills to endure hardship* . *Mayo Clinic* . Retrieved from https://www.mayoclinic.org/tests-procedures/resilience-training/in-depth/resilience/art-20046311

Chapter 3: Practical Self-Care Strategies

Practical Self-Care Strategies

Imagine waking up every day feeling refreshed, balanced, and ready to tackle whatever comes your way. This sense of well-being is not a distant dream but an achievable reality through the practice of self-care. Often misunderstood as mere indulgence, true self-care goes far beyond bubble baths and spa days. It comprises a series of intentional actions aimed at nurturing mental wellness and emotional balance. By paying attention to our needs and dedicating time for ourselves, we can cultivate resilience and joy in our daily lives.

Yet, in our fast-paced world, many struggle to prioritize self-care. The demands of work, family, and societal pressures often leave us feeling overwhelmed and depleted. Activities that once brought pleasure become chores, and taking time for oneself feels like a luxury rather than a necessity. For instance, consider Jane, who used to find solace in painting but now hardly picks up a brush because she's too busy managing her household and career. Or think about Alex, who enjoys hiking but has stopped due to constant work deadlines. These scenarios are all too familiar, leading to a cycle of stress and burnout.

In this chapter, we will explore practical self-care strategies tailored to individual needs. You'll learn how to identify activities that truly bring you peace and happiness while also discovering new ways to revitalize your routine. We'll delve into the importance of balancing physical and mental activities and discuss methods to integrate self-care practices seamlessly into your daily life. By embracing these personalized strategies, you'll be better equipped to face life's challenges with renewed vigor and emotional stability. Let's embark on this journey towards creating a sustainable self-care routine that nurtures your mind, body, and spirit.

Developing a Self-Care Routine Tailored to Individual Needs

When we talk about developing a self-care routine tailored to individual needs, it's essential to start by identifying what truly brings joy and relaxation into your life. Personalizing your self-care practice means you are not just following a generic list of tips; you are digging deep to find out what resonates with you as a unique individual.

To create a personalized self-care plan:

- Begin by reflecting on past experiences. Think about activities that have previously brought you peace or happiness. It could be as simple as a walk in the park, reading a book, listening to your favorite music, or painting.

- Consider trying new activities. Sometimes the routine things we do lose their spark, so exploring new hobbies can inject fresh enthusiasm into your life. This could include joining a dance class, experimenting with cooking, or even journaling.

- Pay attention to both physical and mental activities. A balanced approach helps maintain overall well-being. Keep a mix of activities that enhance your physical health like yoga or hiking, along with those that boost your mental health like meditation or engaging in creative arts.

Prioritizing self-care allows individuals to recharge and better cope with daily stressors and challenges. By making self-care an integral part of your life, you effectively build resilience. Understanding this isn't just about feeling good temporarily but creating a sustainable practice that supports ongoing mental wellness.

This brings us to the idea of experimenting with different self-care practices. Mental well-being is highly personal, and what works wonders for one person might not be as effective for another. Therefore, it's crucial to be open to trying various methods until you discover what fits best for you.

- Start small. Introduce one or two new practices at a time rather than overwhelming yourself with numerous changes. This could mean starting with a five-minute meditation each morning or setting aside ten minutes daily for reading.

- Track your feelings. Keeping a journal of how each self-care activity makes you feel can provide insightful data. Note any changes in mood, energy levels, and general outlook on life.

- Be patient. Adjusting and finding the right blend of activities takes time. Give yourself grace during this exploratory phase and recognize that some practices may need tweaking to better suit your needs.

Consistency and commitment to self-care routines are key to reaping long-term benefits. Self-care isn't a quick fix; it's an ongoing commitment to yourself because you genuinely matter. Here's how you can cultivate consistency:

- Schedule it in. Just as you would with any other important appointment, make sure to block off time for self-care in your calendar. This ensures that it becomes a non-negotiable part of your day.

- Set realistic goals. It's vital to set practical and attainable goals. Committing to 30 minutes of exercise three times a week is more achievable than aiming for an hour every day if you're starting from zero.

- Create accountability. Share your self-care goals with friends or family members who can offer support and encouragement. Alternatively, join online communities where you can share your progress and gain motivation.

The key takeaway here is that tailoring self-care to personal preferences and needs enhances its effectiveness in promoting emotional balance. Our society often glamorizes busyness and productivity, sometimes at the expense of our mental health. Breaking away from this narrative is essential. Movement towards self-care doesn't imply neglecting responsibilities but rather ensuring that you have the strength and mental clarity to handle them efficiently.

In today's fast-paced world, integrating mHealth technologies can further support your self-care routine. Apps and wearable devices can help monitor aspects such as sleep patterns, diet, and physical activity, providing valuable insights into your well-being. An intriguing development in nursing models emphasizes the role of these technologies in improving patient outcomes (Choi, 2023). Leveraging such tools can keep you informed and engaged in your self-care journey, offering real-time feedback that can help fine-tune your practices.

Additionally, personalized care planning integrated into routine healthcare has shown promise in enhancing self-monitoring and creating individualized care plans (Eikelenboom et al., 2016). This supports the notion that self-care is not just limited to personal efforts but can be greatly enhanced when synchronized with professional guidance and technology.

Adopting these strategies can significantly impact your mental wellness, making it easier to manage stress and balance emotions effectively. Tailoring self-care routines to fit your unique preferences allows you to create a nurturing environment where you thrive. As we advance in understanding self-care through both traditional and modern lenses, it's clear that prioritizing ourselves is not just beneficial but necessary for a well-rounded, happy life.

Remember that this journey is deeply personal and subjective. What works splendidly for one person might need adjustments for another. The goal is to explore, experiment, and ultimately establish routines that promote your emotional and mental well-being.

So, begin today with small, intentional steps. Reflect on what brings joy, try new activities, commit to consistent practices, and don't hesitate to utilize technological aids that align with your preferences. Before you know it, you'll find yourself in a much better place, mentally balanced, and ready to tackle life's challenges with renewed vigor.

Exploring Mindfulness Techniques for Stress Reduction

Mindfulness techniques offer us a lifeline in our often chaotic lives. They present an opportunity to pause, breathe, and ground ourselves in the present moment —a powerful antidote for stress and anxiety. Research by the American Psychological Association has shown that mindfulness meditation can positively alter brain structure and function (APA, 2019). By practicing mindfulness, we train our attention to focus on what's happening here and now, which is profoundly calming and centering.

One of the simplest yet most effective mindfulness practices is mindful breathing. It encourages us to concentrate solely on our breath, observing each inhalation and exhalation without judgment. This practice can be as brief as a few minutes or longer, depending on what we need in the moment. To start, find a quiet space and sit comfortably:

- Close your eyes and take a deep breath in through your nose, allowing your abdomen to expand.

- Slowly exhale through your mouth, letting go of any tension.

- Notice the sensation of the air filling your lungs and the release as you exhale.

- If your mind wanders, gently bring your focus back to your breath without self-criticism.

Regular practice of mindful breathing helps cultivate a sense of present-moment awareness—an invaluable tool for reducing anxiety and enhancing emotional well-being.

Building on this foundation, consistent mindfulness exercises can further improve our emotional regulation and resilience. Studies have highlighted that mindfulness-based interventions, such as Mindfulness-Based Stress Reduction (MBSR), are particularly effective in decreasing levels of stress and improving emotional health (Elliott et al., 2021). These interventions involve structured programs that integrate mindfulness practices into our daily routines, making them accessible regardless of how busy our schedules may be.

For those eager to integrate more mindfulness into their life, consider the following practices:

- Start with short, daily mindfulness sessions. Even five minutes of focused meditation can make a significant difference.

- Incorporate mindfulness into routine activities. While brushing your teeth, washing dishes, or walking, engage fully with the sights, sounds, and physical sensations of the task.

- Use guided mindfulness apps or online courses to stay consistent. There are numerous resources designed to support sustained practice.

As mindfulness becomes a regular part of our lives, we observe not only improved emotional regulation but also a notable increase in self-compassion and acceptance. This shift fosters a positive outlook and promotes mental clarity.

The beauty of integrating mindfulness into everyday activities lies in its simplicity and profound impact. When we routinely bring mindful awareness to our actions, it reduces rumination on negative thoughts and heightens mental clarity. For instance, taking a mindful approach to eating—savoring each bite and being fully present during meals—can transform a mundane activity into a rich, sensory experience. Here's how we can make this a habit:

- Begin each day with a mindful intention. Take a moment upon waking to set a clear, positive intention for your day.

- Schedule regular breaks for mindfulness practice. Short pauses throughout the day help reset your focus and reduce accumulated stress.

- End your day with reflection. Spend a few minutes acknowledging the day's events with gratitude and self-compassion.

Overall, incorporating mindfulness practices into our lives equips us with tools to manage stress and maintain emotional balance. As we become more adept at noticing and accepting our thoughts and feelings without judgment, we build resilience against life's inevitable challenges. This nurturing of mental wellness and emotional balance is not just about enduring stress but thriving despite it.

In essence, mindfulness empowers us, providing a shield against the relentless pressures of modern life. Through mindful breathing, regular practice, and integrating mindfulness into daily routines, we lay the groundwork for a balanced, peaceful existence. Embracing these practices offers more than just immediate relief—it cultivates a sustainable path towards lasting emotional well-being and inner peace.

The Importance of Proper Nutrition and Physical Activity in Mental Health

When it comes to self-care practices for nurturing mental wellness and emotional balance, incorporating proper nutrition and regular physical activity cannot be overstated. These elements lay the groundwork for a robust mind and energetic body, providing essential benefits that ripple out into almost every area of life.

Nutrient-dense foods provide critical foundations for a healthy mind and body. This isn't just about filling up our stomachs but ensuring that what we consume is packed with the right nutrients to support our mood regulation and cognitive function. Our brains need an array of vitamins and minerals, such as vitamin B, magnesium, and omega-3 fatty acids, to operate optimally. Research has shown a clear link between nutrient deficiencies and mental health issues (Grave, 2020).

Here's what you can do to achieve this:

- Integrate whole foods like fresh vegetables, fruits, lean proteins, and grains into your diet.

- Prioritize foods rich in omega-3 fatty acids like fish, walnuts, and flaxseeds.

- Avoid processed foods and added sugars which can lead to spikes and crashes in energy and mood.

- Stay hydrated, as even mild dehydration can impair brain function and mood.

On the other hand, regular physical activity plays a pivotal role in mental well-being by releasing endorphins, the body's natural "feel-good" hormones, and reducing levels of stress hormones such as cortisol (Live Another Day, 2022). This isn't just about hitting the gym vigorously; moderate activities like walking, yoga, or cycling can also significantly enhance your mental state.

To reap these benefits:

- Find an activity you enjoy. Whether it's dancing, hiking, or simply taking brisk walks, the key is consistency.

- Aim for at least 30 minutes of exercise most days of the week. This can be broken down into shorter intervals if needed.

- Incorporate variation to keep yourself engaged. Mixing cardio with strength training or stretching routines can prevent boredom.

- If you're new to regular exercise, start slowly to avoid burnout and gradually increase intensity and duration as your fitness improves.

Moreover, balancing your diet and exercise routines doesn't just contribute to your physical health; it has a profound impact on sleep quality, energy levels, and mental clarity. A balanced approach ensures that as your body gets stronger, your mind remains alert and peaceful.

Engaging in both proper nutrition and physical activities as part of your self-care routine helps create a sustainable lifestyle that supports mental wellness. It's clear that what we fuel our bodies with and how we move them directly affects our capacity to manage stress, stay focused, and maintain emotional equilibrium (Agrawal et al., 2023).

By making small, manageable changes – like replacing sugary snacks with nuts and fruits or taking a short walk during your lunch break – you build a foundation of habits that nourish your mind and body alike. Integrating these practices into your daily life doesn't have to be overwhelming; it's about embracing small, consistent actions that collectively make a significant difference.

It's crucial to emphasize that self-care isn't a one-size-fits-all concept. What works for one person might not work for another, and that's perfectly okay. The journey to better mental wellness through nutrition and physical activity is personal, requiring some trial and error to find what best suits your unique needs and preferences.

For many, the barriers to implementing these practices can feel daunting. Time constraints, budget concerns, and lack of motivation are common obstacles. However, there are strategies to navigate these challenges effectively:

- Planning meals ahead of time can streamline grocery shopping and ensure you always have healthy options available.

- Physical activity doesn't require an expensive gym membership. Community resources like parks, online workout videos, and local walking groups can provide accessible options.

- Pairing up with friends or joining support groups can add a social element to your new routines, making them more enjoyable and less burdensome.

Ultimately, nourishing your body with the right foods and moving it regularly should be viewed as non-negotiable components of your self-care regimen. They serve as powerful tools to maintain and elevate your mental health, empowering you to face life's demands with resilience and grace. By prioritizing these aspects, you invest in a healthier, happier future for yourself.

Remember, every step towards incorporating these habits, no matter how small, is progress. Celebrate each milestone, listen to your body, and be patient with yourself. Sustainable change takes time, but the rewards – improved mood, better sleep, enhanced cognitive function, and overall well-being – are well worth the effort.

So, take that first step today. Choose a nutritious snack, plan your next meal, or set aside some time for a walk. Each action, no matter how minor it may seem, contributes to a larger picture of health and happiness. In this complex dance of life, let nutrition and physical activity be your dependable partners, guiding you towards a harmonious balance of mind and body.

Creating Boundaries and Practicing Self-Compassion in Daily Life

Creating boundaries and practicing self-compassion in daily life

Establishing personal boundaries is not just about restricting others; it's a fundamental act of self-preservation and respect. By setting clear limits, you can protect your mental well-being, foster healthier relationships, and prevent the emotional drain that often comes from overextending yourself. Imagine having a protective shield that deflects unnecessary stress and negative energy, allowing only positive aspects to penetrate your space.

Here's how you can set effective boundaries:

- Start by identifying areas where you feel overwhelmed or taken advantage of. This could be at work, with family, or among friends.

- Communicate your limits clearly and assertively without feeling guilty. For instance, if you need uninterrupted time to focus on a project, let your colleagues know this in advance.

- Practice consistency. Once you've set a boundary, stick to it. This reinforces your commitment to self-respect and helps others understand your limits.

- Finally, allow room for flexibility. Boundaries are not walls but guidelines that can be adjusted as circumstances change.

Setting boundaries might initially feel uncomfortable, especially if you're used to being overly accommodating. However, this practice ultimately serves both parties by laying down a foundation of mutual respect and understanding.

In parallel to establishing boundaries, nurturing self-compassion plays a crucial role in maintaining a balanced emotional state. Being kind and gentle with oneself during tough times is not an indulgence but a necessity. Often, people fall into the trap of harsh self-criticism when things go wrong or when they face challenges. Instead, imagine treating yourself as you would a dear friend—offering words of encouragement instead of judgment.

Self-compassion involves three main components: self-kindness, recognition of our common humanity, and mindfulness. Self-kindness means being warm towards oneself even in the face of failure. It's understanding that imperfection is a natural part of being human. Recognition of common humanity allows us to see our experiences as part of the larger human condition, reducing feelings of isolation. Mindfulness involves maintaining a balanced awareness of our emotions, neither suppressing them nor letting them overwhelm us.

This inner shift towards kindness significantly impacts resilience and fosters a positive self-image. Empirical studies have shown that individuals who practice self-compassion tend to exhibit greater psychological health, reduced anxiety, and enhanced coping mechanisms (Crego et al., 2022).

Empowering oneself to say no is another vital step in upholding mental health. Many people grapple with the fear of disappointing others or appearing selfish when they refuse requests or decline invitations. However, saying no is a powerful affirmation of one's priorities and well-being. It's about recognizing your limits and valuing your needs just as much as you value the needs of others.

Steps to practice saying no effectively:

- Assess the request against your current commitments and emotional capacity.

- Respond honestly. If you can't commit to something, express this calmly without over-explaining.

- Suggest alternatives if you're comfortable, like rearranging the task for a later time or delegating it to someone else.

- Trust your instincts. If something doesn't feel right, it's okay to decline without guilt.

The ability to say no is intrinsically linked to mental fortitude and self-respect. It allows you to conserve energy and allocate it towards endeavors that genuinely matter to you. This, in turn, strengthens your overall emotional resilience and prevents burnout.

Cultivating self-compassion has far-reaching effects on mental health and overall well-being. When you're compassionate towards yourself, you build a reservoir of internal support that buffers against life's inevitable setbacks. This nurtures a resilient spirit and cultivates a more optimistic outlook, contributing to a stable and enduring sense of self-worth.

For example, research confirms that practicing self-compassion leads to increased happiness, improved emotional regulation, and reduced instances of depression and anxiety (Neff, 2024). It's important to dispel the myth that self-compassion is synonymous with self-indulgence or weakness. In fact, self-compassionate individuals often demonstrate higher levels of personal responsibility and perseverance.

Engaging in self-care practices like setting boundaries and embracing self-compassion doesn't require grand gestures. Small, consistent actions can create significant positive changes over time. Implementing these strategies may mean taking short breaks throughout your day to reset, speaking kindly to yourself when faced with setbacks, or carving out quiet moments for meditation or reflection. Each small act of self-care reinforces your commitment to your own well-being.

Incorporating these practices into your daily life equips you with tools to manage stress, maintain balance, and foster a healthier relationship with yourself and others. It's about creating a sustainable approach to living where your mental and emotional health take precedence. By doing so, you're not only enhancing your quality of life but also contributing positively to the lives of those around you.

Ultimately, establishing boundaries and practicing self-compassion are not just individual acts; they contribute to a larger culture of empathy and respect. When you take care of yourself, you bring a more centered and compassionate self to your interactions, thereby enriching your personal and professional relationships. So, give yourself permission to prioritize your needs, extend compassion inwardly, and enjoy the profound benefits that follow.

Embracing Holistic Self-Care for Lasting Well-Being

Reflecting on the importance of implementing self-care practices to nurture mental wellness and emotional balance, we recognize that the journey to well-being is deeply personal. Throughout this chapter, we've explored how a tailored self-care routine can protect our mental health, cultivate resilience, and foster a more balanced life.

We started by discussing the need to personalize self-care routines based on what truly brings us joy and relaxation. Reflecting on your past experiences and trying new activities were identified as key steps in finding what resonates with you. We've seen that prioritizing both physical and mental activities significantly enhances our overall well-being, creating a harmonious balance between body and mind.

We also touched upon the necessity of experimenting with different self-care methods. By starting small, tracking your feelings, and being patient, you can discover the activities that best support your mental wellness. Consistency in these practices is vital for reaping long-term benefits. Scheduling self-care, setting realistic goals, and creating a network of accountability are foundational steps toward making self-care an integral part of daily life.

The integration of technology, like mHealth apps and wearable devices, presents modern avenues to support and refine your self-care habits. These tools help monitor various aspects of your health, providing real-time feedback and professional guidance that can enhance your self-care efforts.

It's essential to understand that self-care is not merely about individual actions but involves establishing boundaries and practicing self-compassion. Setting clear limits in your relationships and workplace helps shield you from unnecessary stress, while self-kindness during challenging times strengthens your inner resilience. The ability to say no effectively is equally crucial, empowering you to prioritize your needs without guilt.

Incorporating proper nutrition and regular physical activity into your self-care routine further supports mental health. Consuming nutrient-rich foods and engaging in physical activity contribute to better mood regulation, cognitive function, sleep quality, and energy levels. Small, incremental changes in diet and exercise habits can create significant positive impacts over time.

As we've navigated through these concepts, the central theme emerges: Self-care is a multifaceted practice that encompasses personalized activities, boundary setting, self-compassion, and healthy living. It's not just a temporary fix but a sustainable lifestyle choice that promotes ongoing mental wellness and emotional balance.

The broader implication of embracing self-care extends beyond individual well-being. When you prioritize your mental health, you're better equipped to handle life's challenges, contributing positively to your environment. This ripple effect fosters a healthier, more empathetic community where individuals support and uplift each other.

So, as you continue your journey towards nurturing mental wellness, remember that self-care is a deeply personal and evolving process. Start with small, intentional steps, reflect on what brings you joy, explore new practices, and remain committed to consistency. Utilize technology wisely and don't hesitate to seek professional guidance. With patience and dedication, you'll cultivate a self-care routine that nurtures not just your mind but your entire being, paving the way for a balanced and fulfilling life.

Remember, at the heart of self-care is the acknowledgment that you matter—your well-being matters. Embrace this journey with an open heart, and let it lead you to a place of peace and resilience.

References

Choi, S. (2023). *Personal Health Tracking: A Paradigm Shift in the Self-Care Models in Nursing* . *JMIR Nursing* , 6(1), e50991. https://doi.org/10.2196/50991

American Psychological Association. (n.d.). *Mindfulness meditation: A research-proven way to reduce stress* . Retrieved from https://www.apa.org/topics/mindfulness/meditation

Kriakous, S. A., Elliott, K. A., Lamers, C., Owen, R. (2021). *The effectiveness of mindfulness-based stress reduction on the psychological functioning of healthcare professionals: a systematic review* . *Nature Publishing Group* , 1(12), 1-21. DOI: 10.1007/s12671-020-01500-9

APA citation:

Mahindru, A., Patil, P., & Agrawal, V. (2023). *Role of Physical Activity on Mental Health and Well-Being: A Review* . *Cureus* , 15(1), 10.7759/cureus.33475. https://doi.org/10.7759/cureus.33475

Bartlett, L., Buscot, M-J., Bindoff, A., Chambers, R., & Hassed, C. (2021). *Mindfulness Is Associated With Lower Stress and Higher Work Engagement in a Large Sample of MOOC Participants* . *Frontiers in Psychology* , 12, article 724126. https://doi.org/10.3389/fpsyg.2021.724126

Crego, A., Yela, J. R., Riesco-Matías, P., Gómez-Martínez, M.-Á., Vicente-Arruebarrena, A., & Daily, K. (2022). *The Benefits of Self-Compassion in Mental Health Professionals: A Systematic Review of Empirical Research* . *Psychology Research and*

Behavior Management , 15, 2599. https://doi.org/10.2147/PRBM.S359382

Live Another Day. (2022). *The Link Between Nutrition, Fitness & Mental Health* . *Live Another Day* . Retrieved from https://liveanotherday.org/resources/nutrition-fitness/

Eikelenboom, N., van Lieshout, J., Jacobs, A., Verhulst, F., Lacroix, J., van Halteren, A., Klomp, M., Smeele, I., & Wensing, M. (2016). *Effectiveness of personalised support for self-management in primary care: a cluster randomised controlled trial* . *The British Journal of General Practice* , 66(646), e354. https://doi.org/10.3399/bjgp16X684985

Neff, K. (n.d.). *What is Self-Compassion?* . Self-Compassion. Retrieved from https://self-compassion.org/what-is-self-compassion/

Coulter, A., Entwistle, V. A., Eccles, A., Ryan, S., Shepperd, S., & Perera, R. (2015). *Personalised care planning for adults with chronic or long-term health conditions.* The Cochrane Database of Systematic

Reviews, 3. https://doi.org/ 10.1002/14651858.CD010523.pub2

Dalle Grave, R. (2020). *Nutrition and fitness: Mental health* . *Nutrients* , 12(6), 1804. https://doi.org/ 10.3390/nu12061804

Chapter 4: Building Emotional Resilience

Building Emotional Resilience

Ever notice how some people seem to glide through life's storms, emerging stronger and even more driven? That's the magic of emotional resilience. It's like a secret superpower that allows individuals not just to survive, but truly thrive, in the face of adversity. Imagine being able to navigate life's unexpected twists and turns with a sense of calm and confidence, knowing that no matter what happens, you have the tools to handle it. Emotional resilience isn't about ignoring the tough times but about finding ways to stay grounded and hopeful when things get rough.

Life is inherently unpredictable, throwing curveballs our way when we least expect them. These challenges can stem from various sources—losing a job, enduring a breakup, facing health issues, or simply dealing with daily stressors. Without emotional resilience, such events can feel overwhelming, leading to mental fatigue and despair. For example, someone who has lost their job might experience intense feelings of worthlessness and anxiety. On the flip side, a person equipped with emotional resilience would acknowledge their emotions, analyze the situation, seek solutions, and view the setback as a stepping stone rather than an insurmountable barrier. This doesn't mean they don't feel the weight of the problem; instead, they possess the ability to bounce back and maintain a positive outlook.

In this chapter, we delve into the intricacies of building emotional resilience. We begin by exploring how acknowledging and managing emotions can prevent them from destabilizing our mental well-being. You'll discover practices like mindfulness and deep-breathing exercises that help center your thoughts and reduce stress. As we move forward, we'll discuss the significance of embracing change, setting boundaries, and maintaining self-care routines—all crucial elements in strengthening your resilience. Additionally, we'll highlight the importance of fostering supportive relationships and seeking professional help when needed. By the end of this chapter, you'll be equipped with practical strategies and insights to enhance your resilience, paving the way for long-term well-being and a more fulfilling life.

Understanding Emotional Resilience

When life throws us curveballs, having emotional resilience can make all the difference. It's about more than just enduring hardship—it's about thriving despite it. Emotional resilience is the ability to bounce back from adversity and maintain a positive outlook even when things get tough. This skill is critical for long-term well-being and mental health.

One of the main tenets of emotional resilience is recognizing and managing our emotions effectively. Emotions are powerful forces that, if left unchecked, can wreak havoc on our mental state. Here's a framework for developing this crucial skill:

- **Acknowledge Your Emotions** : The first step is to become aware of what you're feeling. Name the emotion. Is it anger, sadness, frustration? Recognizing what you're experiencing is fundamental.

- **Understand the Root Cause** : Dig into why you feel the way you do. Is it due to a specific event or accumulated stressors?

- **Practice Mindfulness** : Engage in activities like meditation or deep-breathing exercises. These can help center your mind and let go of negative thoughts.

- **Express Yourself** : Whether through journaling, talking with a friend, or creative outlets like art, expressing your feelings helps mitigate their intensity.

- **Seek Professional Help if Needed** : Sometimes, we need guidance from mental health professionals who can offer strategies tailored to our individual needs (Mayo Clinic, 2023).

Resilience also means adapting to change and navigating life's uncertainties with greater ease. Change is often uncomfortable, but it's a constant in life. Those who build resilience embrace change rather than resist it. They learn to see new opportunities in changing landscapes. Imagine sailing across an ever-shifting sea; instead of battling the waves, you adjust your sails to move forward.

Developing resilience further involves practicing self-care, seeking support when needed, and utilizing coping strategies during difficult times. Resilience isn't about solitary strength—it's about fostering relationships and leaning on others as you navigate challenges. It's akin to building a community within yourself that values self-compassion and external connections.

Practicing self-care is essential for building resilience. Self-care goes beyond indulging in a spa day; it encompasses a variety of practices that nurture your physical, mental, and emotional health. Here's how you can incorporate self-care into your routine:

- **Prioritize Physical Health** : Maintain a balanced diet, get regular exercise, and ensure you get adequate sleep. Physical wellness lays the groundwork for mental fortitude.

- **Engage in Relaxation Techniques** : Activities such as yoga, meditation, and deep breathing can ease the mind and reduce stress levels.

- **Set Boundaries** : Learn to say "no" to activities or commitments that drain your energy. Guard your time and mental space diligently.

- **Pursue Hobbies** : Spend time on activities that bring you joy and allow you to unwind.

In addition to self-care, seeking support and utilizing coping strategies are indispensable components of resilience. Connecting with others provides emotional sustenance and broader perspectives. Don't hesitate to reach out to friends, family, or support groups. Sometimes, sharing your burden can halve it, making your problems seem more manageable.

Utilizing effective coping strategies also plays a significant role. Coping strategies are techniques you can use to face and overcome stressful situations. Practical strategies include:

- **Problem-Solving** : Break down large problems into smaller, manageable tasks. Create a plan and tackle each step methodically.

- **Positive Visualization** : Imagine a successful outcome to the issue you're facing. Visualizing success can boost your confidence and motivation.

- **Distraction** : Engage in activities that divert your mind from stress. Reading, exercising, or engaging in hobbies can provide much-needed respite.

- **Emotional Release** : Sometimes, allowing yourself to cry or vent frustration can be cathartic. Don't bottle up your emotions.

- **Professional Assistance** : There's no shame in seeking therapy or counseling. Trained professionals can offer invaluable tools and perspectives (APA, n.d.).

Cultivating emotional resilience takes commitment and practice, but the rewards—a stronger, more adaptable you—are well worth the effort. It allows you to handle stress, maintain your mental health, and lead a fulfilling life despite the obstacles you face. In essence, resilience furnishes you with the tools to shape your narrative positively, no matter the circumstances.

As you continue this journey toward greater resilience, remember to treat yourself kindly. Life's challenges are inevitable, but your response to them is within your control. By nurturing your emotional resilience, you empower yourself not just to survive, but to thrive amidst adversity.

Embracing these facets of resilience doesn't mean you'll never experience hardship or distress again. Rather, it equips you with the strength to face these challenges head-on and emerge stronger. Each setback becomes a stepping stone, each disappointment a lesson learned.

So, embark on this journey with patience and compassion for yourself. Understand that resilience is not a fixed trait, but a set of skills that can be cultivated over time. With each step forward, no matter how small, you are building your capacity for resilience—and in turn, paving the way for a healthier, more robust future.

Adapting to Change and Overcoming Adversity

Resilience is a remarkable quality that allows us to adapt to change and bounce back from adversity. It's like an inner strength that can be nurtured, helping you navigate the storms of life and emerge stronger. Embracing change, rather than resisting it, plays a critical role in developing this resilience. When we see change as an opportunity for growth, we're better positioned to adapt and thrive.

Imagine every change as a doorway to personal development. Instead of shutting down in the face of new challenges, view them as adventures that can teach you something valuable. It's essential to remind yourself that while change can be uncomfortable, it also brings fresh experiences and perspectives. By embracing the unknown, you open yourself up to growth that would otherwise remain out of reach.

Here is what you can do in order to achieve the goal:

- Approach changes with curiosity rather than fear.

- Reflect on past changes that led to positive outcomes.

- Set small, achievable goals that align with the new circumstances.

- Use each experience as a learning opportunity to build your skills and knowledge.

Another cornerstone of building resilience is how we perceive setbacks. Resilient individuals have the ability to view setbacks as temporary hurdles rather than insurmountable barriers. This mindset shift allows them to focus on solutions rather than dwelling on problems. Understanding that adversity is often transient can empower you to take proactive steps towards overcoming it.

When faced with a setback, remind yourself that this too shall pass. Take a step back, breathe, and assess the situation calmly. Instead of ruminating on what went wrong, channel your energy into figuring out what can be done next. Ask yourself constructive questions like, "What can I learn from this?" or "What are my options moving forward?"

Here is what you can do in order to achieve the goal:

- Reframe negative thoughts by focusing on temporary aspects of the challenge.
- Identify practical solutions and create an action plan.
- Surround yourself with positive affirmations and reminders of previous successes.
- Practice gratitude to shift your focus from what's lacking to what you have.

Building a strong support network and practicing self-care are instrumental in enhancing your resilience. When you have a solid foundation of people who care about you, coping with adversity becomes more manageable. Likewise, prioritizing your physical and mental health ensures you're in the best shape to face life's challenges.

Cultivating relationships with empathetic and understanding individuals is key. These connections provide emotional support when you need it most, reminding you that you're not alone. On the flip side, taking time for self-care activities like exercise, adequate sleep, and mindfulness practices strengthens your overall well-being. This balance between external support and internal self-care creates a sturdy framework for resilience.

Here is what you can do in order to achieve the goal:

- Reach out to trusted friends and family regularly.

- Join community groups or online forums that share your interests.

- Schedule regular self-care activities, such as exercise, meditation, or hobbies you enjoy.

- Limit your exposure to negative influences and environments.

Effective problem-solving skills and a positive mindset form the final piece of the resilience puzzle. Being able to tackle problems head-on and maintain optimism helps ensure that setbacks don't derail you entirely. A positive mindset doesn't mean ignoring reality but rather choosing not to be paralyzed by it.

When encountering a problem, break it down into smaller, manageable parts. Look at the issue from different angles and brainstorm potential solutions. Stay flexible and be willing to adjust your plans as needed. Coupled with maintaining a hopeful outlook, this approach keeps you grounded and motivated, even in tough times.

Connecting all of these strategies underscores one clear takeaway: developing resilience involves embracing change, staying flexible, and approaching challenges with a growth-oriented mindset. It's not about avoiding difficulties but rather facing them head-on with the belief that you can endure and grow through them.

Cultivating a Positive Mindset

Positive thinking can enhance emotional resilience by reframing setbacks as learning opportunities and focusing on strengths. Life, as we know it, is riddled with moments that challenge our fortitude and test our limits. Yet, how we mentally navigate these obstacles plays a pivotal role in shaping our overall well-being. Picture this: a child learning to ride a bicycle for the first time. They fall, scrape their knee, and pick themselves up again. With each attempt, they become better at balancing and pedaling until they eventually master the skill. That's the power of positive thinking in action. By seeing each setback not as a failure but as a stepping-stone towards success, they build resilience.

Here's what you can do in order to achieve the goal:

- Begin by acknowledging your feelings about the setback without judgment. Recognize any negative emotions or thoughts before reshaping them.

- Reflect on past experiences where you overcame difficulties and emerged stronger. Use these moments as personal evidence of your ability to persist.

- Break the situation down into manageable parts. Identify specific areas where you have control and focus on actionable steps you can take.

- Surround yourself with positive affirmations and motivational reminders. This could be through journaling, vision boards, or even setting daily intentions.

- Lastly, celebrate small victories. Each progress, no matter how minute, deserves acknowledgment.

Practicing gratitude and mindfulness fosters a positive mindset, promoting resilience and emotional well-being. It's fascinating how such simple practices can make profound differences in our lives. Gratitude helps us shift our focus from what we lack to what we have, creating a mindset geared towards abundance rather than scarcity. Mindfulness, on the other hand, keeps us anchored in the present, allowing us to experience life fully without the weight of past regrets or future anxieties.

To harness the benefits of gratitude:

- Start a gratitude journal. Daily jot down three things you're thankful for, regardless of how big or small they are.

- Express your gratitude to others directly. Send thank-you notes, messages, or verbally acknowledge someone's positive impact in your life.

- Practice mindful breathing. Take a few minutes each day to sit quietly, breathe deep, and center your mind on the present.

Cultivating self-compassion and self-awareness helps individuals maintain a positive outlook and cope with challenges effectively. Self-awareness is about understanding your thoughts, emotions, and behaviors in various situations. Through self-compassion, we learn to treat ourselves kindly, especially during times of failure or suffering, much like how we would support a dear friend experiencing similar struggles. This internal kindness nurtures our resilience and provides a solid foundation for bouncing back.

Steps to develop self-compassion and self-awareness include:

- Spend time reflecting on your emotional responses to different events in your life. Journaling can be an effective tool for this purpose.

- Engage in positive self-talk. Whenever you notice self-critical thoughts, consciously replace them with kinder, more supportive statements.

- Practice meditation focused on self-compassion. Visualization techniques, where you imagine sending yourself love and care, can be particularly helpful.

- Learn to set boundaries and assertively voice your needs. Knowing when to say "no" and communicating it clearly can protect your mental wellbeing.

- Seek feedback from trusted friends or mentors. Sometimes others can provide insights into behaviors or patterns you might not easily recognize in yourself.

Engaging in activities that bring joy and fulfillment can uplift mood and contribute to a positive outlook on life. What brings joy to one person may differ significantly from another, but the underlying principle remains universal: joy boosts our spirit and enriches our lives. Whether it's through hobbies, social interactions, or simply taking time to relax, these joyful experiences rejuvenate us and serve as buffers against life's adversities.

Here is how to incorporate joy-inducing activities:

- Identify hobbies or activities that you genuinely enjoy. This could range from painting, gardening, playing sports, to reading. Allocate dedicated time to engage in these activities regularly.

- Connect with others who share your interests. Joining clubs, groups, or online communities can provide both enjoyment and a sense of belonging.

- Make room for spontaneity. Sometimes unplanned activities can bring unexpected joy and create memorable experiences.

- Incorporate nature into your routine. Spending time outdoors, whether it's a walk in the park or hiking, can have therapeutic effects.

- Allow yourself downtime. In our busy lives, scheduling periods of rest and relaxation is crucial for maintaining balance and preventing burnout.

Overall, the practice of nurturing a positive mindset isn't about ignoring life's difficulties. Instead, it's about cultivating a resilient attitude that empowers us to thrive despite challenges. As we've explored, strategies like positive thinking, practicing gratitude and mindfulness, self-compassion, and engaging in joyful activities are invaluable tools for enhancing our resilience.

It's essential to remember that building resilience is a journey, not a destination. There will be days when setbacks feel overwhelming, and maintaining a positive outlook seems impossible. During such times, leaning on the tools and practices discussed can act as an anchor, grounding you and providing the strength needed to persevere. Evidence suggests that these practices are more than just feel-good strategies—they have been shown to improve psychological and physical health (Mayo Clinic, 2023).

In a world often fraught with uncertainties and pressures, fostering emotional resilience becomes indispensable. The ability to bounce back, adapt, and grow from life's inevitable challenges leads not only to emotional well-being but also to a richer, more fulfilling life. Let's embark on this path together, committed to nurturing our minds, hearts, and spirits with kindness, patience, and unwavering resilience.

Practical Strategies for Emotional Regulation

Enhancing resilience to overcome challenges and setbacks for long-term well-being is a journey, not a one-time fix. It involves managing and regulating emotions effectively to maintain emotional balance and resilience in the face of life's inevitable ups and downs. Let's delve into some practical strategies that can help on this path.

Developing emotional intelligence is a powerful way to enhance resilience. Emotional intelligence is the ability to understand, use, and manage your emotions in positive ways. It helps you relieve stress, communicate effectively, empathize with others, overcome challenges, and defuse conflict.

To build emotional intelligence:

- **Observe your emotions:** Make it a habit to notice what you're feeling throughout the day. Label your emotions accurately – are you really angry, or are you frustrated? This mindfulness creates an internal awareness that is crucial for emotional regulation.

- **Consider the impact of your emotions:** Reflect on how your emotions influence your thoughts and actions. Recognize patterns that negatively affect your behavior and decision-making.

- **Practice empathy:** Try to see things from others' perspectives. Understanding and feeling someone else's emotions can increase your connection and reduce negative emotions like anger and frustration.

Utilizing relaxation techniques like deep breathing or meditation can significantly help regulate emotions and reduce stress levels. These methods calm the body and mind, making it easier to tackle challenges with a clear head.

Here's how you can start incorporating these techniques:

- **Deep Breathing:** Sit comfortably, close your eyes, and take slow, deep breaths. Focus on the rise and fall of your chest, letting each breath relax your body more deeply.

- **Meditation:** Find a quiet space and set aside a few minutes each day. Focus on your breath, a mantra, or guided meditations available through apps or online resources. The goal isn't to stop thinking but to allow thoughts to come and go without judgment.

- **Mindfulness:** Practice paying full attention to the present moment. This might involve noticing the taste, texture, and aroma of food you're eating or the way your feet feel as they touch the ground during a walk.

Setting boundaries and engaging in self-care practices are also essential to promoting emotional well-being and resilience. Boundaries protect your energy and mental health by setting limits on what you can tolerate and giving you more control over your life. Self-care is about taking deliberate steps to maintain your health and well-being.

To set effective boundaries and practice self-care:

- **Know your limits:** Identify what drains your energy and what feels overwhelming. Understand your physical, emotional, and psychological limitations.

- **Communicate clearly:** Express your limits and needs to others in a respectful but firm manner. For example, if you're feeling overwhelmed at work, let your supervisor know that you need to prioritize certain tasks over others.

- **Prioritize self-care:** Make time for activities that recharge you, whether it's reading, exercising, spending time in nature, or enjoying a hobby. Ensure you get enough sleep, eat nutritious meals, and stay hydrated.

Seeking support from loved ones or mental health professionals can be invaluable in managing emotions during difficult times. Connection with others provides a safety net during challenging periods. Loved ones can offer perspective, comfort, and advice, while professionals can provide tools and strategies tailored to your unique situation.

When you need to reach out:

- **Talk openly:** Share your feelings with trusted friends or family members. Sometimes, just expressing what you're going through can lighten the emotional load.

- **Seek professional help:** A therapist or counselor can offer coping mechanisms, therapeutic strategies, and an objective understanding of your situations. They can assist in developing a precise plan to enhance resilience.

- **Join support groups:** Connecting with people experiencing similar challenges can provide mutual encouragement and practical advice. Look for local or online groups that focus on issues you're facing.

Effectively managing emotions is a key component of emotional resilience. When we handle our emotions well, we foster stability and adaptive coping mechanisms for long-term well-being. Each strategy we've discussed plays an important role in this broader goal.

Developing emotional intelligence not only enhances resilience but also improves every aspect of our interactions with others. Utilizing relaxation techniques allows us to approach stressful situations with a calmer, more centered mindset. Setting boundaries and engaging in self-care reaffirm our worth and ensure we have the energy and strength needed to navigate life's hurdles. And seeking support reminds us that we do not have to face our struggles alone; there is power in community and professional guidance.

Remember, building resilience is an ongoing process. It involves making consistent efforts to understand and manage your emotions, engage in self-care, and draw strength from your relationships. By implementing these strategies, you're not just enhancing your resilience but actively investing in your long-term well-being. Life will always present challenges, but with these tools, you'll be better equipped to face them head-on and emerge stronger on the other side.

Wrap-Up: Strengthening Your Emotional Core

Having navigated through strategies like emotional regulation, self-care, and seeking support, it's clear that enhancing resilience is an ongoing journey. A key point discussed was the recognition and effective management of emotions, which is foundational to bouncing back from life's inevitable challenges. By acknowledging our feelings, understanding their root causes, and employing mindfulness techniques, we create a stable internal environment to face adversities confidently.

Reflecting on the idea introduced earlier in the chapter, building resilience isn't about solitary strength. It's about fostering connections and leaning on others when needed. This interconnectedness helps us navigate change gracefully and adapt without feeling isolated. Just as we've explored, viewing setbacks as temporary hurdles rather than insurmountable barriers is vital to maintaining forward momentum.

Our current position emphasizes that while we can't control life's curveballs, we can control our response. Embracing change with curiosity and a growth-oriented mindset transforms daunting experiences into opportunities for learning and personal development. The importance of practicing self-care —through physical health, relaxation techniques, and setting boundaries—cannot be overstated. These self-care practices ensure we're in the best shape mentally and physically to handle stress.

Moreover, what should concern readers is the tendency to overlook emotional well-being until it becomes overwhelming. Ignoring mental health often leads to prolonged suffering, making challenges seem insurmountable. Recognizing this can prompt action before reaching a breaking point—seeking timely support, engaging in fulfilling activities, and maintaining a positive outlook all contribute significantly to resilience.

On a broader scale, cultivating emotional resilience has profound consequences. It doesn't just impact individual lives but also contributes to healthier communities. Resilient individuals can support others, creating a ripple effect leading to a more emotionally balanced society.

As we move forward, remember that each small step towards resilience builds a foundation for long-term well-being. Challenges will arise, but your response molds your experience. Treat yourself with kindness, patience, and compassion. Life's journey is filled with uncertainties, yet by nurturing your resilience, you empower yourself to face them head-on and thrive.

References

HelpGuide.org. (n.d.). *Surviving tough times by building resilience* . Retrieved from https:// www.helpguide.org/articles/stress/surviving-tough-times.htm

Brook Lane Health Services. (n.d.). *Resilience: Building a Positive Mindset.* https://www.brooklane.org/blog/resilience-building-positive-mindset

Mayo Clinic. (2023). *Resilience: Build skills to endure hardship* . Retrieved from https://www.mayoclinic.org/tests-procedures/resilience-training/in-depth/resilience/art-20046311

American Psychological Association. (n.d.). *Resilience guide for parents and teachers* . https://www.apa.org/topics/resilience/guide-parents-teachers

No author information available. (n.d.). *Cultivating resilience: Strategies for building mental strength and coping with life's challenges* . Empathy HQ. https://www.empathyhq.org/blog/cultivating-resilience-strategies-for-building-mental-strength-and-coping-with-lifes-challenges

Davis, M. C. (2009). *Building emotional resilience to promote health* . *American Journal of Lifestyle Medicine* , 3(1 Suppl), 60S. https://doi.org/10.1177/1559827609335152

Artuch-Garde, R., González-Torres, M. C., de la Fuente, J., Vera, M. M., Fernández-Cabezas, M., & López-García, M. (2017). *Relationship between resilience and self-regulation: A study of Spanish youth at risk of social exclusion* . *Frontiers in Psychology* , 8. https://doi.org/10.3389/fpsyg.2017.00612

Mayo Clinic. (2023). *Positive thinking: Stop negative self-talk to reduce stress* . Retrieved from https://www.mayoclinic.org/healthy-lifestyle/stress-management/in-depth/positive-thinking/art-20043950

American Psychological Association. (n.d.). *Building your resilience* . Retrieved from https://www.apa.org/topics/resilience/building-your-resilience

Harvard Business Review. (2010). *How to Bounce Back from Adversity* . *Harvard Business Review* . https://hbr.org/2010/01/how-to-bounce-back-from-adversity

Chapter 5: Mind-Body Connection

Mind-Body Connection

Imagine feeling a tight knot in your stomach when faced with stress or experiencing a surge of energy and happiness after a good workout. These moments are more than just fleeting sensations; they reveal the intricate dance between our minds and bodies. Our emotions, thoughts, and physical states are entwined in ways we often overlook but profoundly affect our overall well-being. This mind-body connection is not just a poetic idea but a scientifically grounded concept that underscores the need for a holistic approach to health.

Consider the widespread issue of chronic stress. When life's pressures mount, our bodies respond in various ways—from persistent headaches and digestive problems to a weakened immune system. It's not uncommon to hear someone say their stress makes them sick, and there's truth behind this sentiment. Stress hormones like cortisol can wreak havoc on our bodies' natural balance, leading to many physical ailments. Conversely, positive mental states can act as a balm for our bodies. Feelings of joy, contentment, and optimism have been linked to reduced inflammation and improved heart health, demonstrating how closely intertwined our emotional and physical states are.

In this chapter, we delve deeper into the profound link between mental and physical health. We will explore the impact of stress and anxiety on the body and how positive mental states can enhance physical well-being. Practical strategies like mindfulness meditation, regular physical activity, balanced nutrition, and quality sleep will be discussed, providing actionable steps to nurture both mind and body. By understanding and embracing the mind-body connection, you will be better equipped to achieve holistic wellness and lead a more harmonious life.

The Impact of Mental State on Physical Health

Exploring the interconnectedness of mental and physical health for holistic well-being reveals a profound truth: our state of mind is intrinsically linked to our body's condition, and vice versa. It's a dance that significantly influences overall wellness and vitality.

Consider the impact of mental stress and anxiety on our physical health. It's not just an emotional burden; it translates into real physical symptoms. People under constant stress often report headaches, digestive disturbances, and even a weakened immune system. This isn't merely an anecdotal observation but a well-documented phenomenon in scientific literature (Bradley University Online, 2018). When mental distress becomes chronic, it can result in ongoing physical ailments, creating a vicious cycle that's hard to break.

On the flip side, positive mental well-being offers astounding benefits for physical health. Feeling optimistic and content doesn't just make life more enjoyable—it reduces inflammation, enhances immune responses, and promotes a general sense of vitality. A meta-analysis by Harvard University found that optimism could correlate with cardiovascular health and decrease the progression of heart disease (Bradley University Online, 2018). Simply put, nurturing a positive mindset can have your body singing along in harmony.

Bridging mental and physical health means understanding their symbiotic relationship. Addressing mental health concerns doesn't just clear the mind; it can lead to tangible improvements in physical health outcomes. Research indicates that individuals who actively engage in mental health services tend to experience better physical health because they are more likely to maintain healthy behaviors, like regular exercise and balanced nutrition (WebMD, n.d.). Of course, the reverse is also true—taking care of your physical health can significantly brighten your mental outlook. Regular check-ups, staying active, and mindful eating go a long way in keeping both mind and body in sync.

Practices like mindfulness meditation serve as powerful tools to bridge this mind-body connection. By quieting the mind and focusing on the present, meditation helps individuals become more attuned to their bodies. This awareness fosters a deeper sense of well-being that radiates through all aspects of life. Here's how you can integrate mindfulness meditation into your daily routine:

- Start by setting aside a few minutes each day in a quiet space where you won't be interrupted.

- Sit comfortably with your back straight, close your eyes, and focus on your breath.

- As you breathe in and out, let your thoughts flow without judgment, gently bringing your attention back to your breath when your mind wanders.

- Over time, gradually increase the duration of your sessions as you become more comfortable.

- Consider using guided meditations or apps that offer structured programs to help deepen your practice.

These small steps can create a meaningful shift in your perception and response to stress, ultimately promoting a harmonious balance between your mental and physical health.

Understanding the intertwined relationship between mental and physical health emphasizes the importance of a holistic approach to well-being. Rather than treating issues in isolation, recognizing the interplay between mind and body leads to more effective and comprehensive care strategies. If you're struggling mentally, it's crucial to seek support—not just for the sake of your mind but for your overall physical health. Similarly, adopting healthy lifestyle habits like regular exercise, a wholesome diet, and proper sleep positions you to enjoy a resilient and joyful life.

Let's reflect on the direct impacts of stress on the body. Chronic stress has been shown to elevate cortisol levels, which in turn affects various bodily systems including the immune response, metabolism, and even brain function (Agrawal et al., 2023). Elevated cortisol can lead to conditions such as hypertension, obesity, and type 2 diabetes. These physical conditions then feed back into the stress cycle, worsening mental health. However, identifying these stress-induced patterns early allows for intervention through healthier coping mechanisms like physical activity or social engagement.

Equally important is recognizing how enhancing positive emotions can bring about physiological benefits. Positive mental states have been associated with lowered risks of cardiovascular diseases and improved longevity (Bradley University Online,

2018). Encouragingly, engaging in activities that boost happiness and satisfaction—whether it's hobbies, social interactions, or volunteerism—promotes a robust immune function and keeps inflammation at bay. Such activities aren't just feel-good exercises; they are scientifically backed methods to sustain both mental and physical resilience.

Let's delve deeper into practical lifestyle changes. Physical activity is a cornerstone of this holistic approach. Exercise not only improves fitness but also plays a critical role in boosting mental health. Activities like running, swimming, or brisk walking release endorphins—the body's natural mood lifters—which can ease symptoms of depression and anxiety (Agrawal et al., 2023). Regular exercise routines improve self-esteem, cognitive function, and emotional regulation, essential components of mental well-being.

Nutrition also cannot be overlooked. A balanced diet rich in fruits, vegetables, lean proteins, and whole grains provides the nutrients necessary for optimal brain and body function. Omega-3 fatty acids, found in fish and flaxseeds, are particularly beneficial for brain health. Avoiding excessive processed foods and sugars prevents energy crashes and mood swings, fostering stable mental and physical energy.

Quality sleep is another critical element. Inadequate sleep affects mood, cognitive performance, and physical health. Establishing good sleep hygiene, like maintaining a consistent bedtime, creating a restful environment, and limiting screen time before bed, ensures restorative sleep that supports both mental clarity and physical vigor.

Lastly, never underestimate the power of community and relationships. Social connections can act as buffers against the stresses of life. Engaging in meaningful conversations, sharing experiences, and participating in group activities foster a sense of belonging and shared purpose, amplifying mental and emotional support networks.

In conclusion, appreciating the deep connection between mental and physical health encourages a more integrated approach to personal well-being. By acknowledging how our mental state influences physical health—and vice versa—we can adopt practices that nurture both, laying a foundation for a healthier, happier life. Practicing mindfulness, maintaining an active lifestyle, following a balanced diet, prioritizing sleep, and fostering social bonds are vital steps toward achieving holistic wellness. It's not just about living longer—it's about living better.

Integrating Relaxation Techniques into Daily Life

Integrating relaxation techniques into our daily routines can significantly enhance both mental wellness and physical health. It's fascinating how interconnected our mind and body truly are. When we think about overall well-being, it's essential to consider both aspects holistically rather than individually.

Deep breathing exercises and progressive muscle relaxation offer a pragmatic starting point for integrating relaxation into your routine. Both of these methods are supported by substantial research showing their effectiveness in reducing stress hormones and promoting a relaxed state throughout the body and mind (Mayo Clinic, 2024).

Here is what you can do to incorporate deep breathing exercises:

- Find a quiet place where you won't be disturbed.
- Sit or lie down in a comfortable position.
- Begin by taking a slow, deep breath through your nose, allowing your lower belly to rise as your lungs fill with air.
- Hold your breath for a count of four.
- Exhale slowly through your mouth, feeling your lower belly fall.
- Repeat this process for several minutes.

Progressive muscle relaxation can also be a helpful tool:

- Start by sitting or lying down in a comfortable position.

- Focus on one muscle group at a time, beginning with your toes.

- Tense the muscles in your toes for about five seconds, then release for 30 seconds.

- Gradually move up your body, focusing on each muscle group, from your toes to your neck and head.

Engaging in activities like yoga or tai chi is another excellent way to improve flexibility, strength, and mental clarity, while also reducing tension and promoting relaxation. These practices have been shown to effectively harmonize the mind and body, creating a sense of peace and well-being. Yoga incorporates postures, known as asanas, along with breath control, which can help calm the nervous system (Mayo Clinic, 2024). Tai chi, with its flowing movements and focus on controlled breathing, provides similar benefits.

If you're new to these practices, start small. Attend a beginner's class or follow online tutorials designed for newcomers. Commit to practicing for just ten to fifteen minutes a day, gradually increasing the duration as you become more comfortable. The key is consistency, not intensity, and ensuring that each session leaves you feeling more relaxed than when you began.

Connecting with nature can also rejuvenate the mind and body. Nature exposure has been linked to a reduction in stress and an increase in feelings of well-being. Something as simple as a walk in the park, gardening, or even sitting by a window looking out at trees can make a significant difference. Multiple studies have shown that spending time outdoors in green spaces reduces cortisol levels—a marker of stress—and boosts mood.

As modern life keeps us increasingly indoors, making a conscious effort to spend time outside is crucial. Aim to spend at least 20 minutes in nature daily. This could mean anything from having your morning coffee on the patio to scheduling weekend hikes. These moments not only foster a sense of peace but also allow you to disconnect from digital devices, giving your mind a much-needed break.

Creating a calming bedtime routine is also vital for better sleep quality, which is essential for both mental and physical health. Poor sleep can exacerbate stress, anxiety, and depression, while quality sleep can boost your resilience and mood. A good night's rest starts well before you hit the pillow.

Here is what you can do to establish a relaxing bedtime routine:

- Set a consistent sleep schedule by going to bed and waking up at the same time every day, even on weekends.

- Create a pre-sleep ritual that signals your body it's time to wind down. This could include activities such as reading a book, taking a warm bath, or practicing gentle stretches.

- Limit exposure to screens at least an hour before bed, as the blue light emitted by phones and computers can interfere with melatonin production.

- Make your bedroom a sanctuary for sleep: keep it cool, dark, and quiet, and invest in comfortable bedding.

Incorporating these relaxation techniques into daily life can yield profound benefits. By managing stress effectively, you're likely to experience improved mental clarity and enhanced overall well-being. Relaxation isn't just a luxury; it's a necessary component of a healthy lifestyle.

By integrating deep breathing exercises, progressive muscle relaxation, yoga, and tai chi into your routine, and by spending time in nature along with maintaining a calming bedtime routine, you can create an environment where mental and physical health thrive together.

It's important to remember that relaxation techniques are skills that require practice and patience. You might not see results immediately, but persistence will pay off. The journey to holistic well-being is a personal and ongoing process, but with commitment and routine, the positive changes you'll experience can be life-transforming.

For anyone struggling with mental health issues, these techniques can act as valuable tools in managing symptoms and improving overall quality of life. Bear in mind that while these strategies can help significantly, they may be most effective when used in conjunction with professional advice and treatment. So, if you're finding it particularly challenging, don't hesitate to seek support from a healthcare provider. Remember, your well-being includes recognizing when you need a little extra help and being open to receiving it.

The Role of Sleep Quality in Mental Wellness

Quality sleep is crucial for cognitive function, emotional regulation, and overall mental well-being. This might seem like common knowledge, but the ripple effects of poor sleep extend far deeper than just feeling groggy or irritable. Consider the findings of a study conducted among final-year university students in China: those with poor sleep quality exhibited significantly higher levels of negative psychological well-being, such as anxiety and depression, compared to their peers who enjoyed regular, restful sleep (Gao et al., 2018).

When we're deprived of sleep, our brains struggle with tasks that demand sharp thinking, problem-solving skills, and emotional resilience. The research supports this, indicating that insufficient sleep can magnify feelings of sadness or stress, which over time can build up to more severe mental health conditions like depression or anxiety disorders (Sleep Foundation, 2020). To put it into perspective, proper sleep acts as the foundation upon which our mental and emotional stability rests.

Creating a consistent sleep schedule and bedtime routine can signal to the body that it's time to rest, improving sleep quality. If you're aiming to set a regular sleep pattern, here's what you can do:

- Go to bed and wake up at the same times every day, even on weekends. Consistency helps regulate your internal clock.

- Develop a pre-sleep routine that's relaxing. This might include reading a book, taking a warm bath, or listening to calming music.

- Avoid heavy meals and caffeine before bedtime. These can interfere with falling asleep and staying asleep.

- Use your bed only for sleep and intimacy. Make it a space solely associated with rest to reinforce the connection between bed and sleep.

Our bodies thrive on routine, and creating a scheduled approach to sleep allows us to take advantage of this natural inclination. It's akin to planting seeds in a garden: if done at the right time and cared for with consistency, the results are fruitful.

Limiting screen time before bed and creating a comfortable sleep environment can enhance relaxation and promote better sleep. Screens emit blue light, which interferes with our brains' ability to produce melatonin, the hormone responsible for inducing sleep. To minimize this disruption:

- Turn off electronic devices at least an hour before bed. Opt for activities that don't involve screens, like reading or journaling.

- Use blue light filters on your devices if you must use them before bed.

- Ensure your sleep environment is conducive to rest. This means a cool, dark, and quiet room. Invest in blackout curtains if street lights or morning sun disrupts your sleep. A good mattress and pillows that support your sleep posture can also make a significant difference.

Think of your bedroom as a sanctuary tailored to rest. Free from distractions and designed with comfort in mind, it becomes a place where falling asleep happens naturally and without effort.

Practicing mindfulness or relaxation techniques before bed can help calm the mind and prepare the body for restful sleep. Mindfulness isn't just about achieving a state of zen; it's about quieting the mind and allowing it to transition smoothly into a state of rest. Here's how you can incorporate these practices into your nightly routine:

- Engage in deep breathing exercises. Focused, slow breathing can help reduce stress and signal to your body that it's time to wind down.

- Try progressive muscle relaxation. This involves tensing and then slowly releasing each muscle group, starting from your toes and moving up to your head.

- Practice meditation. Even a few minutes of mindfulness meditation, where you focus on your breath and dismiss any intrusive thoughts, can significantly impact sleep quality.

- Use guided imagery. Close your eyes and imagine a peaceful scene – it could be a beach, forest, or any tranquil setting – and let your mind wander there until you fall asleep.

These practices might feel unfamiliar at first, but with persistence, they become second nature. They serve as the gentle nudge your mind needs to shift gears from the hustle of daily life to the tranquility of sleep.

Prioritizing good sleep hygiene plays a vital role in maintaining mental wellness and overall health. Good sleep hygiene encompasses all the habits and practices mentioned above, but it's worth reiterating that making small adjustments can lead to significant improvements in how we sleep.

In summary, quality sleep isn't just a luxury—it's a necessity for mental and physical well-being. Recognizing the profound effect sleep has on our cognitive functions and emotional equilibrium shifts its importance from the periphery to the core of our health strategies. By establishing consistent routines, creating conducive environments, and incorporating mindful practices, we aren't merely addressing sleep issues; we are fostering a foundation for a healthier, happier life. In a world bustling with stimuli and responsibilities, dedicating time and effort to improve our sleep may very well be the most impactful step we can take toward holistic well-being.

Holistic Approaches to Enhance Mind-Body Connection

The interconnectedness of mental and physical health is a cornerstone of holistic well-being. It's an intricate dance where the mind influences the body, and the body reflects the state of the mind. For those who have struggled with mental health issues or are looking to heal from past trauma, understanding and nurturing this connection can be immensely beneficial.

Yoga is one of the most profound practices that encompasses both the physical and mental realms of our being. It combines physical postures, breathwork, and meditation to promote relaxation, flexibility, and mental focus. Imagine starting your day with a simple sun salutation. As you move through each pose, your muscles stretch and strengthen, yet the sequence also encourages deep, mindful breathing. This combination not only warms up your body but also calms your mind, creating a sense of centeredness and readiness for the day ahead.

To begin incorporating yoga into your daily life:

- Start with gentle movements. Try simple poses like child's pose or cat-cow, focusing on your breath.

- Gradually introduce more dynamic sequences like sun salutations or warrior poses as your comfort and confidence grow.

- Integrate short meditation sessions at the end of your practice to absorb the benefits fully.

Meditation, another pillar of holistic wellness, cultivates mindfulness, awareness, and emotional regulation. These practices foster a deeper connection between the mind and body, which can be transformative. Take, for instance, a few minutes of focused breathing. By sitting quietly and observing your breath, your mind starts to settle. You become more aware of your thoughts and emotions without getting entangled in them. This awareness extends beyond the meditation mat and into your daily life, helping you respond to stress and challenges with greater clarity and calmness.

Steps to establish a meditation routine:

- Find a quiet, comfortable space where you won't be disturbed.

- Start with just five minutes of focusing on your breath, gradually increasing the time as you feel more comfortable.

- Use guided meditations if you're new to the practice; they can provide structure and support.

Integrating these holistic practices into daily routines can reduce stress, increase resilience, and improve overall well-being. Stress reduction is crucial because, as research indicates, chronic stress can lead to a host of physical and mental health problems. By setting aside time each day for yoga or meditation, you create a dedicated space for self-care. This intentional act can lower cortisol levels, enhance mood, and even improve immune function (Woodyard, 2011).

For daily integration:

- Schedule your practice at a consistent time each day, making it part of your routine.

- Begin with shorter periods to avoid feeling overwhelmed, then slowly extend the duration as you find your rhythm.

- Reflect on how these practices impact your mood and energy levels, adjusting as needed to suit your lifestyle.

Engaging in activities that promote the mind-body connection, such as tai chi or qigong, can also enhance balance, coordination, and mental clarity. Both tai chi and qigong consist of slow, deliberate movements combined with mindful breathing. These practices might not seem physically strenuous, but they require a high level of concentration and control, effectively bridging the gap between mental and physical exercise.

To incorporate mind-body activities:

- Explore local classes or online tutorials to get started with basic movements.

- Practice regularly, even if only for a few minutes each day, to help build muscle memory and enhance coordination.

- Listen to your body; these practices should leave you feeling invigorated, not exhausted.

The science supporting these benefits is robust. Various studies have shown that yoga improves strength, balance, and flexibility, while also benefiting heart health by reducing inflammation and stress levels (expert et al., 2021). Additionally, regular meditation practice has been linked to enhanced emotional regulation and reduced symptoms of anxiety and depression (American Osteopathic Association, 2021).

Understanding these concepts is vital for anyone aiming to improve their mental and physical health. When we prioritize holistic practices, we're not just treating symptoms; we're fostering a sustainable lifestyle that emphasizes wellness in its entirety. Whether it's rolling out a yoga mat or setting up a meditation space, these small steps can lead to significant changes.

In conclusion, incorporating holistic practices like yoga and meditation into your routine isn't just about physical fitness—it's about nurturing your entire being. These practices offer tools to manage stress, enhance mental clarity, and improve overall well-being. Start small, be patient with yourself, and gradually build a routine that supports your journey towards a balanced and healthier life. Remember, the goal is not perfection but progress, and every step you take brings you closer to holistic well-being.

Fostering Holistic Well-Being Through Mind-Body Harmony

Exploring the interconnectedness of mental and physical health has shown us that one profoundly affects the other. As we've discussed, mental stress can manifest in physical ailments, leading to a cycle that can be challenging to break. Conversely, fostering a positive mental state has remarkable benefits for physical well-being.

We began by examining how stress impacts not just our state of mind but also our bodies, causing headaches, digestive issues, and weak immune responses. On the contrary, optimism and contentment contribute to reduced inflammation and better cardiovascular health. This paints a clear picture: nurturing our mental health is not only about feeling better emotionally; it's essential for physical health too.

Connecting mental and physical health means more than just understanding their relationship—it involves taking actionable steps to improve both simultaneously. Engaging in practices like mindfulness meditation allows us to bridge this gap, promoting a harmonious balance between the two. Small, consistent steps—such as setting aside time for deep breathing or progressive muscle relaxation—can have a meaningful impact on reducing stress levels and enhancing overall well-being.

It's also crucial to recognize that while these techniques bring significant benefits, they are part of a broader approach to holistic health. For some, seeking professional help remains a vital piece of their wellness puzzle. Addressing mental health concerns through professional support can lead to tangible improvements in physical health outcomes, encouraging healthier behaviors and lifestyles.

Ultimately, the interconnectedness of our mental and physical health emphasizes the need for a comprehensive approach that addresses both aspects with equal importance. By integrating simple yet powerful practices into our daily lives, we not only respond better to stress but also lay down a solid foundation for lasting well-being. Remember, it's not just about living longer—it's about living better, with a mind and body working in concert to create a joyful, resilient life.

As you reflect on these insights, consider how you might begin implementing small changes today. Perhaps start with just a few minutes of mindfulness or a brief walk in nature. These steps may seem minor, but they can profoundly impact both your mental clarity and physical vitality. The journey towards holistic health is ongoing, and each step brings you closer to a balanced, healthier, and happier life.

References

Scott, A. J., Webb, T. L., Martyn-St James, M., Rowse, G., & Weich, S. (2021). *Improving sleep quality leads to better mental health: A meta-*

analysis of randomised controlled trials . *Sleep Medicine Reviews* , 60, 10.1016/j.smrv.2021.101556. https://doi.org/10.1016/j.smrv.2021.101556

Mahindru, A., Patil, P., & Agrawal, V. (2023). *Role of physical activity on mental health and well-being: A review* . *Cureus* , 15(1), 1-10. https://doi.org/10.7759/cureus.33475

Johns Hopkins Medicine. (2021). *9 Benefits of Yoga* . Retrieved from https://www.hopkinsmedicine.org/health/wellness-and-prevention/9-benefits-of-yoga

Woodyard, C. (2011). *Exploring the therapeutic effects of yoga and its ability to increase quality of life* . *International Journal of Yoga* , 4(2), 49. https://doi.org/10.4103/0973 6131 85485

American Osteopathic Association. (2021). *The benefits of yoga* . *American Osteopathic Association* . Retrieved from https://osteopathic.org/what-is-osteopathic-medicine/benefits-of-yoga/

American Psychiatric Association. (n.d.). *"Just relax."* *While it sounds simple, it is often quite difficult to calm our minds and relax the tension in our bodies.* https://www.psychiatry.org/news-room/apa-blogs/ relaxation-techniques-for-mental-wellness

Zhai, K., Gao, X., & Wang, G. (2018). *The role of sleep quality in the psychological well-being of final year undergraduate students in China* . *International Journal of Environmental Research and Public Health* , 15(12), 2881. https://doi.org/10.3390/ ijerph15122881

Sleep Foundation. (2020). *Mental Health and Sleep* . Retrieved from https://www.sleepfoundation.org/ mental-health

Bradley University Online. (2018). *How Mental Health Affects Physical Health* . Retrieved from https://onlinedegrees.bradley.edu/blog/how-mental- health-affects-physical-health/

WebMD. (n.d.). *How does mental health affect physical health?* Retrieved from https://

www.webmd.com/mental-health/how-does-mental-health-affect-physical-health

North Shore University HealthSystem. (2015). *Benefits of relaxation* . Retrieved from https://www.northshore.org/healthy-you/benefits-of-relaxation/

Mayo Clinic. (2024). *Relaxation techniques: Try these steps to lower stress* . Health information library. Retrieved from https://www.mayoclinic.org/healthy-lifestyle/stress-management/in-depth/relaxation-technique/art-20045368

Chapter 6: Overcoming Negative Thought Patterns

Overcoming Negative Thought Patterns

Have you ever found yourself spiraling into a vortex of negative thoughts, feeling trapped by your own mind? It often starts with a seemingly insignificant worry that quickly snowballs into a series of distressing scenarios. Imagine you're about to meet friends for dinner, and you begin to think, "What if they don't like my outfit?" Before long, you're convinced the evening will be a disaster and they'll never invite you again. This cascade of negativity isn't just taxing; it can significantly impair your mental health and overall well-being.

This phenomenon stems from what's known as cognitive distortions—irrational thought patterns that warp our perception of reality. They act as filters, magnifying negatives and diminishing positives, making situations appear far worse than they truly are. For instance, consider someone who fails to complete one task at work and immediately concludes they're terrible at their job, disregarding all previous accomplishments. Or someone who receives minor feedback and catastrophizes it into an imminent job loss. These thought patterns not only lead to heightened stress and anxiety but can also create a self-fulfilling prophecy of failure and discontent.

In this chapter, we will delve into understanding these cognitive distortions more deeply and explore practical strategies to combat them. We will start by identifying common types of cognitive distortions and provide you with tools to recognize them in your daily life. From there, we will guide you through techniques such as keeping a thought journal, practicing mindfulness, and engaging in cognitive reframing. By the end of this chapter, you will have actionable steps to challenge and reframe your negative thoughts, fostering a healthier and more resilient mindset.

Identifying Cognitive Distortions

Recognizing cognitive distortions is a critical step in fostering mental well-being. These irrational thought patterns can significantly impact our emotions and behaviors, often leading to heightened stress, anxiety, or depression. Think of these distortions as mental filters that twist reality, making situations seem worse than they are. By becoming aware of these patterns, we empower ourselves to challenge and change them, paving the way for a healthier mindset.

Common cognitive distortions range from black-and-white thinking to catastrophizing and personalization. Black-and-white thinking, also known as all-or-nothing thinking, involves viewing situations in extremes without recognizing the gray areas in between. For example, you might think, "If I'm not perfect, I am a complete failure." This rigid perspective overlooks nuances and variations that reflect real-life complexities (Floyd, 2023).

Catastrophizing is another widespread distortion where individuals anticipate the worst possible outcome, often with little or no evidence. Consider someone who receives minor feedback at work and immediately assumes they will be fired. This type of thinking can escalate minor issues into overwhelming crises. Personalization involves taking undue responsibility for events outside one's control, such as believing that if a friend cancels plans, it must be because of something you've done wrong (Dozois et al., 2016).

These cognitive distortions can create a negative loop, reinforcing harmful beliefs and emotions. Understanding these patterns is essential for shifting perspectives and cultivating a more positive mindset. One effective strategy to combat cognitive distortions is keeping a thought journal. This tool helps track negative thoughts and identify recurring themes. When you encounter a triggering situation, write down what happened, your thoughts on it, and how it made you feel. Then, consider alternative perspectives. Ask yourself, "Is this thought based on fact or assumption? Could there be another explanation?"

Mindfulness practices also play a crucial role in identifying and managing cognitive distortions. Mindfulness encourages present-moment awareness without judgment. When we're mindful, we observe our thoughts from a distance rather than getting caught up in them. This practice enables us to recognize distorted thinking patterns and prevent them from influencing our emotions and actions.

Additionally, cognitive reframing techniques can help address these distortions. Reframing involves altering the way we interpret situations, aiming for a more balanced and less negative view. Let's say you have a presentation and think, "I'm going to mess this up and everyone will judge me." Instead, you could reframe it to, "I've prepared well and will do my best; even if I make a mistake, it's not the end of the world."

Here is what you can do in order to achieve this reframing:

- Start by identifying the negative thought.

- Question the accuracy of this thought and explore other possible interpretations.

- Replace the negative thought with a more balanced one.

- Reflect on how this new perspective changes your feelings about the situation.

Engaging in cognitive-behavioral therapy (CBT) with a mental health professional can provide further support in challenging and restructuring distorted thoughts. CBT focuses on altering negative thinking patterns and developing healthier behavioral responses. A therapist guides you through recognizing cognitive distortions, evaluating their validity, and replacing them with more constructive thoughts. Research has shown that CBT is highly effective in treating various mental health conditions, including depression and anxiety (MD, 2022).

Incorporating these strategies into daily life empowers individuals to break free from the cycle of negative thinking and move towards a more positive and resilient mindset. It takes practice and patience, but the benefits are profound. By addressing cognitive distortions head-on, we open the door to improved mental health and overall well-being.

When we become adept at challenging cognitive distortions, we start to experience a shift in our emotional landscape. Situations that once seemed insurmountable begin to appear manageable. Our self-esteem improves as we learn to see ourselves and our accomplishments more accurately and compassionately.

Moreover, addressing cognitive distortions can drastically enhance our relationships. When we stop personalizing others' actions and avoid jumping to conclusions, we communicate more effectively and maintain healthier connections. This shift not only benefits our emotional health but also nourishes our social support systems, which are vital for long-term happiness and stability.

Interestingly, humor can also serve as a coping mechanism for dealing with cognitive distortions. Studies have found that adaptive humor styles, such as affiliative and self-enhancing humor, are negatively correlated with cognitive distortion frequency. In contrast, maladaptive humor styles, like aggressive and self-defeating humor, are positively associated with cognitive distortions and depressive symptoms (Dozois et al., 2016). Incorporating humor into our lives, particularly the types that uplift and connect us with others, can mitigate the impact of negative thinking.

The journey to combating cognitive distortions is ongoing, requiring continuous effort and self-reflection. It's important to remember that progress may come in small increments, and setbacks are a natural part of the process. However, each moment of awareness and each restructured thought brings us closer to a healthier, more fulfilling state of mind.

For those struggling significantly, seeking the guidance of a mental health professional can be an invaluable step. Therapists bring expertise and an objective perspective that can accelerate the process of identifying and overcoming cognitive distortions. Whether through individual therapy, group sessions, or supportive online communities, connecting with others who share similar goals can provide encouragement and accountability.

In summary, recognizing and reframing cognitive distortions is a powerful tool for improving mental wellness. By becoming aware of these irrational thought patterns and employing strategies like thought journals, mindfulness, and cognitive reframing, we can foster a healthier, more positive mindset. Engaging in CBT and incorporating humor can further support this transformation. Remember, every step taken towards challenging these distortions is a step towards greater emotional resilience and overall well-being.

Practicing Cognitive Restructuring and Positive Self-Talk

Imagine you're in a garden. Some parts might look a bit wild and unruly, overgrown with weeds. But if you gently pull out the weeds and plant beautiful flowers in their place, the garden transforms into a peaceful, vibrant space. Your mind works in a similar way. By practicing cognitive restructuring, you can tend to your mental garden, removing the harmful weeds of negative thoughts and planting seeds of balanced, realistic alternatives.

Cognitive restructuring is the process of questioning and changing those negative thought patterns that hold us back. For example, suppose you find yourself thinking, "I'll never be good enough." This thought isn't just unhelpful; it's often unfounded. By challenging it, you can start replacing it with something more balanced, like, "I've faced challenges before and come through them; I can handle this too."

Here is what you can do in order to achieve this:

- Start by identifying the specific negative thought you want to change.

- Ask yourself: What evidence do I have for and against this thought?

- Look for alternative explanations or perspectives.

- Replace the original negative thought with a more balanced one.

It's fascinating how impactful this practice can be. According to studies from the Association for Behavioral and Cognitive Therapies, changing our thought patterns can significantly reduce feelings of anxiety and depression (Greeman, 2023).

Positive self-talk works hand-in-hand with cognitive restructuring. It involves using affirming and constructive language to counteract those negative perceptions we often hold about ourselves. Think of it as being your own best friend when you need it the most.

For instance, instead of telling yourself, "I can't handle this," try saying, "I'm doing the best I can, and that's enough." This shift not only boosts your confidence but also makes it easier to face challenges with a positive mindset.

Here's what you can do to incorporate positive self-talk into your daily life:

- Recognize when you're engaging in negative self-talk.

- Pause and take a deep breath.

- Consciously replace negative statements with positive or neutral ones.

This may feel awkward at first, but practice makes perfect. In time, these positive statements will become second nature. A great reference on this topic suggests that positive self-talk can improve performance and enhance self-esteem, providing a buffer against stress (n.d., 2017).

Visualization exercises, daily affirmations, and gratitude practices are excellent ways to foster a more positive internal dialogue. Visualization can be as simple as picturing yourself succeeding in an area where you currently struggle. Daily affirmations involve repeating positive statements about yourself, such as "I am worthy" or "I am capable."

Gratitude practices, on the other hand, encourage you to focus on what you are thankful for, shifting your perspective from what's lacking to what's abundant. Each evening, jot down three things you're grateful for. As you do this regularly, you'll find that it becomes easier to maintain a positive outlook.

Again, it's helpful to follow some steps:

- Begin your day with a few minutes of visualization, seeing yourself navigate through your day successfully.

- Write down a couple of affirmations that resonate with you and repeat them throughout the day.

- End your day by noting down what you're grateful for, even if they're small things.

Cultivating self-compassion and self-kindness is perhaps the most crucial element in fostering a mindset of acceptance and self-encouragement. It's easy to be hard on ourselves, especially when we face setbacks or when things don't go as planned. However, treating ourselves with the same kindness we would offer a friend can make a world of difference.

Imagine you didn't meet a goal you set for yourself. Instead of beating yourself up, ask yourself, "What would I say to my best friend if they were in this situation?" More likely than not, you'd be supportive and encouraging. Extend that same kindness to yourself.

To cultivate self-compassion, consider these steps:

- Notice when you're being self-critical. Awareness is the first step to change.

- Reframe your inner critic's voice to sound more like a compassionate friend.

- Practice mindfulness; accept your feelings without judgment and reassure yourself that it's okay to feel this way.

- Remind yourself that failure and imperfection are part of the human experience.

Empathy towards oneself nurtures resilience and promotes mental health. It's not just about feeling better—it's about building a foundation of self-worth and self-respect.

In conclusion, cognitive restructuring, positive self-talk, visualization exercises, and cultivating self-compassion all work synergistically to promote a healthier mindset. Remember, it's all about progress, not perfection. By integrating these practices into your daily routine, you can gradually transform the way you think about yourself and your experiences.

So take a moment today to challenge a negative thought, replace it with something kinder, visualize a success, affirm your worth, and show yourself some compassion. Your mental garden awaits your tender care.

Developing a Growth Mindset

Promotion of a healthier mindset requires shifting how we perceive and respond to challenges. Adopting a growth mindset — seeing challenges as opportunities for growth rather than roadblocks — can be instrumental in this transformation.

Imagine you've worked incredibly hard on a project, investing countless hours and thought into each detail. When you finally present it, the reception is lukewarm, and you receive feedback suggesting significant improvements. At this moment, it's easy to feel disheartened or even defeated. After all, isn't putting in the effort supposed to guarantee success? But if we reframe this situation through the lens of a growth mindset, an entirely different perspective emerges.

A growth mindset views challenges as opportunities for learning and development rather than setbacks or failures. Instead of seeing the feedback as a mark against your competence, view it as a valuable insight that highlights areas for improvement. Carol Dweck, a renowned psychologist, describes in her research that individuals with a growth mindset embrace challenges, persist through obstacles, learn from criticism, and draw inspiration from the success of others (School of Education Online, 2020). This attitude transforms every challenge into an opportunity for personal and professional growth.

Cultivating resilience, perseverance, and a belief in one's capacity for growth and improvement forms the bedrock of embracing a growth mindset. It's about nurturing the conviction that abilities and intelligence can develop over time. Resilience allows us to bounce back from setbacks, perseverance keeps us moving forward despite difficulties, and the belief in our capacity for growth encourages us to keep trying new things, even when they seem daunting.

Strategies such as reframing setbacks as learning experiences, seeking feedback for growth, and setting realistic goals are essential tools to support the development of a growth mindset. Here's what can help:

- Reframing setbacks: Instead of viewing a mistake as a failure, consider it a step in the learning process. Each misstep is a chance to gain insights and improve.

- Seeking feedback: Actively seek constructive criticism and use it to identify areas that need refinement. Rather than taking feedback personally, see it as guidance towards improvement.

- Setting realistic goals: Establish short-term, attainable goals that build up to larger objectives. Breaking down goals into smaller, manageable steps ensures steady progress.

Engaging in activities that push you out of your comfort zone is another powerful way to reinforce a growth-oriented perspective. Embrace projects or tasks that intimidate you and challenge yourself to step beyond familiar boundaries. This practice not only enhances skill development but also builds confidence in your ability to tackle new challenges. Here are some actions you can take:

- Volunteer for projects outside your usual scope of work or expertise.

- Join groups or workshops focused on skills you want to develop.

- Challenge yourself with new hobbies or interests that require learning and adaptation.

Adopting a growth mindset fosters resilience and a positive outlook on challenges. Rather than fearing failure, those with a growth mindset see each setback as a stepping stone towards mastery. This perspective not just applies to career and educational pursuits but can profoundly impact overall mental well-being. Recognizing that growth comes through effort and persistence helps mitigate the fear of failure and reduces anxiety about making mistakes.

One of the most empowering aspects of a growth mindset is the realization that talent and intelligence are not fixed traits. By cultivating a belief in one's ability to learn and adapt, individuals unlock a world of potential growth. Knowing that effort and dedication can lead to improvement empowers us to take on new challenges with enthusiasm and optimism. This belief stands at the heart of continued personal development and self-improvement.

In conclusion, reframing negative thoughts and developing a growth mindset opens the door to a more fulfilling and resilient approach to life's challenges. By viewing obstacles as opportunities, embracing resilience and persistence, adopting strategic practices for continuous improvement, and pushing ourselves beyond comfort zones, we lay the foundation for ongoing personal and professional development. Through this transformative mindset, we not only enhance our capabilities but also foster a healthier, more optimistic outlook on life.

So next time you encounter a setback, remember: it's not a testament to your limitations but an invitation to grow.

Embracing Gratitude and Perspective Shifts

Gratitude and perspective play significant roles in reshaping the way we view our lives, especially when negativity seems to cloud our mental landscape. Interestingly, practicing gratitude isn't just about having good manners or saying thank you now and then; it's a powerful habit that can shift your entire mindset.

Practicing gratitude is about more than acknowledging the positive aspects of life—it fosters an overall optimistic outlook. When we focus our attention on what we appreciate, it actually rewires our brain to notice and value these things more frequently.

The relationship between gratitude and improved mental health has been thoroughly studied. According to research, consciously counting blessings can lead to increased happiness and less depression (Greater Good, n.d.). This practice encourages us to shift our focus from what's lacking or problematic to what we already have and cherish, creating a snowball effect of positivity in our daily lives.

Shifting your perspective involves looking at situations through different lenses and reframing negative events constructively. By changing the way we interpret experiences, we can reduce their emotional sting and find opportunities for growth and learning amidst challenges.

Here's how you can start:

- **Identify negative thoughts:** Begin by noticing the negative thoughts that pop up during your day. They could be recurring themes like feeling inadequate at work or dreading social interactions. Writing these thoughts down can help make them tangible and easier to address.

- **Respond to those thoughts:** Replace them with something more positive. If you catch yourself thinking, "I always mess up at my job," rephrase it to, "I've completed projects successfully before, and I can do it again."

- **Chunking:** Break overwhelming tasks into smaller, manageable steps. Instead of stressing over cleaning the entire house, start with one room.

- **Step outside of yourself:** Consider how you would advise a friend dealing with similar thoughts. Often, we are kinder and more rational when advising others than when dealing with ourselves (Lifespan Blog Team, 2022).

Techniques such as keeping a gratitude journal, engaging in acts of kindness, and finding silver linings in challenges are practical ways to cultivate a mindset of gratitude and positivity.

To maintain a gratitude journal:

- Take a few minutes each day, either in the morning or before bed, to jot down three things you are grateful for. These don't have to be grandiose — even appreciating a warm cup of coffee or a kind word from a colleague counts.

- Reflect on why these things made you feel grateful. This deepens your appreciation and strengthens the positive emotions associated with them.

Engaging in acts of kindness can also shift your focus outward and create a ripple effect of positivity. Whether it's helping a neighbor with groceries or simply smiling at a stranger, small gestures can uplift both you and those around you.

Mindfulness practices, focusing on the present moment, and practicing non-judgment are excellent tools to develop a balanced and open mindset.

Here are some steps:

- **Incorporate mindfulness into your daily routine:** Set aside a few minutes every day to focus on your breath and observe your thoughts without judgment. This helps ground you in the present and reduces the tendency to ruminate on past negatives or future anxieties.

- **Practice non-judgment:** When a negative thought arises, acknowledge it without labeling it as 'bad' or trying to push it away. Simply notice the thought and let it pass like a cloud drifting across the sky.

Gratitude not only serves as a powerful counterbalance to negative thinking patterns, but it also provides numerous mental and physical health benefits. For instance, regular gratitude practice has been shown to lower rates of depression and anxiety, improve heart health, and enhance overall well-being (UCLA Health, n.d.).

One key takeaway here is that creating a new habit of gratitude doesn't happen overnight. It's a gradual process that builds momentum with consistent practice. But over time, you'll likely find that it becomes an intrinsic part of your daily thought process, offering resilience and a brighter outlook on life.

Mindfulness also supports this journey. By staying present and avoiding harsh self-criticism, you enable yourself to navigate life's ups and downs with greater ease and clarity.

Remember, transforming your mindset is a marathon, not a sprint. With patience and persistence, you'll find that a more positive and grateful perspective can become your natural state.

Fostering a Healthier Mindset Through Awareness and Practice

In this chapter, we've delved into understanding and reshaping negative thoughts to foster a healthier mindset. Whether it's recognizing common cognitive distortions like black-and-white thinking, catastrophizing, or personalization, or employing tools such as thought journals and mindfulness practices, the journey towards positive mental health is both intricate and achievable.

Earlier, we emphasized the importance of acknowledging cognitive distortions as the first step in transforming our mental landscape. This awareness sets the stage for meaningful change— where negative thought patterns are identified and challenged, allowing us to reframe our perspectives more constructively. By integrating techniques like cognitive restructuring and positive self-talk, you can begin replacing harmful beliefs with balanced, realistic ones, promoting emotional resilience and self-compassion.

One crucial concern for readers might be the perseverance required to maintain these practices. Change doesn't happen overnight; it demands continuous effort and self-reflection. You may find it challenging to consistently confront and reframe negative thoughts, especially during low points.

However, remember that every small step forward contributes to long-term growth and well-being. Building these habits gradually will eventually make them second nature, paving the way for sustained mental wellness.

On a broader scale, embracing these techniques can revolutionize not only individual lives but also collective mindsets. When people challenge and transform their negative thoughts, it fosters a culture of empathy, understanding, and mutual support. Those around you will likely notice your newfound positivity and resilience, possibly inspiring them to embark on their own journeys of mental transformation.

As we move forward, it's essential to recognize that this journey is ongoing and dynamic. There will always be new challenges and opportunities for growth. Embrace the process with patience and kindness towards yourself. So, take a moment today to identify a negative thought, explore alternative perspectives, and plant seeds of positivity and balance in your mental garden. Let this practice become a cornerstone of your path towards a healthier, more fulfilling life.

References

Greater Good. (n.d.). *How gratitude changes you and your brain* . Retrieved from https://greatergood.berkeley.edu/article/item/how_gratitude_changes_you_and_your_brain

Lifespan. (n.d.). *Power of positive reframing - A new look at an old issue* . Retrieved from https://www.lifespan.org/lifespan-living/power-positive-reframing-negative-outlook

Counselors for Franconia-Springfield Self-Help Group. (n.d.). *Changing self-talk* . Retrieved from https://cfsselfhelp.org/library/changing-self-talk

UCLA Health. (n.d.). *Health benefits of gratitude* . Retrieved from https://www.uclahealth.org/news/article/health-benefits-gratitude

Academic Success Center. (2019). *Growth Mindset: What it is, and how to cultivate one* . *Academic Success Center* . Retrieved from https://success.oregonstate.edu/learning/growth-mindset

American Psychological Association. (2019). *Treatment for postdisaster distress: A workbook for community-based psychological first aid* . Retrieved from https://www.apa.org/pubs/books/supplemental/Treatment-for-Postdisaster-Distress/Handout-27.pdf

Floyd, E. (2023). *10 Common Types of Cognitive Distortions . Skyland Trail* . Retrieved from https://www.skylandtrail.org/10-common-types-of-cognitive-distortions/

ICPAS. (2018). *5 ways to embrace a growth mindset* . Retrieved from https://www.icpas.org/information/copy-desk/insight/article/digital-exclusive-2018/5-ways-to-embrace-a-growth-mindset

American University. (2024). *How to Foster a Growth Mindset in the Classroom . School of Education Online* . Retrieved from https://soeonline.american.edu/blog/growth-mindset-in-the-classroom/

.Grinspoon, P (2022) *How to recognize and tame your cognitive distortions.*

Harvard Health . Retrieved from https://www.health.harvard.edu/blog/how-to-recognize-and-tame-your-cognitive-distortions-202205042738

ABCTDiviChild. (2023). *Self-Talk and CBT - 2023 Featured Article - ABCT - Association for Behavioral and Cognitive Therapies* . https://www.abct.org/featured-articles/self-talk-and-cbt/

Rnic, K., Dozois, D. J. A., & Martin, R. A. (2016). *Cognitive distortions, humor styles, and depression* . *Europe's Journal of Psychology* , 12(3), 348. https://doi.org/10.5964/ejop.v12i3.1118

Chapter 7: Embracing Change And Personal Growth

Embracing Change and Personal Growth

Navigating life's ever-changing landscape can often feel like steering a ship through unpredictable waters. Imagine standing on the shores, watching the tide come in and out, each wave different from the last. Some days, the sea is calm and inviting; other days, it roars with challenges that seem insurmountable. Just as sailors must adapt to these changing conditions, we too must learn to embrace the ebb and flow of life. Rather than fearing the storms ahead, what if we saw them as opportunities for growth and transformation? The idea may seem daunting, but within each wave lies the potential for discovering new strengths and perspectives.

Change, while a constant companion, can be one of the most challenging aspects of our lives. For instance, consider moving to a new city or starting a new job. These transitions can uproot our sense of stability, leaving us feeling vulnerable and uncertain. The initial stages might be fraught with anxiety and doubt as we navigate unfamiliar territory. On a more personal level, coping with the end of a relationship or adjusting to a significant health diagnosis can test our resilience. These moments demand not only emotional strength but also a willingness to adapt and grow. By understanding that change is an inevitable part of our journey, we can begin to redefine these experiences as opportunities rather than obstacles.

In this chapter, we will explore how embracing change can serve as a catalyst for personal growth and lead to a more fulfilling life. We'll delve into practical strategies for developing flexible thinking, which allows us to approach challenges with a positive mindset. Additionally, we'll discuss the importance of seeking support during transitions and how leaning on others can provide valuable insights and encouragement. Through real-life examples and actionable advice, this chapter aims to equip you with the tools needed to turn life's uncertainties into stepping stones towards a richer, more resilient self.

Navigating Life Transitions

Accepting change as a natural part of life is fundamental to building resilience and adaptability. Imagine life as a flowing river: changes in direction, depth, and speed are inevitable. At times, the water may rush forward with force, carrying you along whether you feel ready or not. Other moments, it might slow down, giving you space to float and reflect.

Life's transitions are much like that river. They might seem tumultuous and challenging at first. But think of them as opportunities to develop strength and flexibility—qualities that help us navigate both smooth and turbulent waters with greater ease. Viewing change as an integral part of our journey allows us to approach it without fear. Instead of resisting, embracing the flow can open new paths and lead to unexpected discoveries.

Developing flexible thinking is key to navigating life's changes with a positive mindset. Picture your mind as a toolbox. If you only have a hammer, every problem looks like a nail. However, a diverse set of tools enables you to handle various situations effectively. Flexible thinking means being open to different solutions and perspectives.

Here is what you can do in order to achieve flexible thinking:

- Start by questioning assumptions. Challenge yourself to see things from other angles.

- Practice mindfulness to become more aware of your thoughts and emotions.

- Engage in activities that stimulate creative thinking, such as reading diverse genres or learning new skills.

- Encourage conversations with people who hold different viewpoints.

These strategies can broaden your mental horizons, making it easier to adapt when life throws you curveballs. Remember, rigid thinking limits possibilities, while a flexible mindset turns obstacles into stepping stones.

Embracing uncertainty fosters personal growth and the discovery of new opportunities. Uncertainty often feels uncomfortable, akin to walking into a dark room. Yet, this darkness holds potential—the potential for growth, learning, and transformation. When we step into the unknown, we invite new experiences and challenges that can shape and refine us.

Think about moments in your life when uncertainty led to something positive. Maybe a career switch resulted in discovering a passion you never knew existed. Or perhaps a move to a new city introduced you to lifelong friends. The beauty of uncertainty is its capacity to reveal layers of ourselves we hadn't explored. Every uncertain situation carries the seed of possibility waiting to be nurtured.

Seeking support from others during transitions can provide valuable perspectives and encouragement. Humans are inherently social creatures; our relationships form the bedrock of our emotional well-being. Just as plants need sunlight and water to thrive, we too need connection and support to flourish.

During times of change, reaching out to friends, family, or professionals can offer comfort and guidance. Here is what you can do to seek support effectively:

- Identify individuals in your life who are supportive and understanding.

- Share your feelings openly and honestly with them, fostering a sense of trust.

- Be proactive in asking for their advice or sharing your struggles.

- Consider joining support groups or seeking professional counseling if needed.

Connecting with others allows us to borrow their strength when ours wanes. Their insights and experiences can also illuminate paths we might not have considered, helping us navigate our own transitions with greater clarity and confidence.

Ultimately, change is inevitable; embracing it can lead to personal growth and new possibilities. Life's unpredictability doesn't have to be a source of stress but rather a catalyst for self-discovery and improvement. By accepting change, developing flexible thinking, embracing uncertainty, and leaning on our support systems, we can transform life's transitions into powerful opportunities for growth.

In this way, each change becomes less of a hindrance and more of a guiding force, steering us toward a life rich in experiences, resilience, and fulfillment.

Setting Meaningful Goals

Embracing Change as a Catalyst for Personal Growth and Transformation Towards a Fulfilling Life

When it comes to setting meaningful goals for personal development and well-being, clarifying your values and aspirations serves as the foundation. Knowing what genuinely matters to you can help steer your life in a direction that feels both fulfilling and authentic. Often, we rush into goal-setting without taking the time to understand our intrinsic motivations, and this can lead to frustration and unmet expectations. Take a moment to reflect on what truly resonates with you—whether it's cultivating deeper relationships, advancing in your career, or pursuing creative passions. This clarity will act as your compass, guiding you towards goals that align with your core self.

Once you've clarified your values and aspirations, it's time to translate those big dreams into actionable steps. Large goals can often feel overwhelming, making it easy to lose motivation or procrastinate. Breaking down these larger ambitions into smaller, manageable tasks can make them feel more achievable and less intimidating. Here is what you can do to successfully break down your goals:

- Start by identifying the ultimate goal you're aiming for.

- Break this goal down into key milestones or phases.

- Further divide these phases into specific actions or tasks.

- Set a timeline for each action, ensuring they are realistic and attainable.

- Prioritize the tasks and focus on one step at a time.

By chunking down your goals, you'll find that progress feels more tangible. Each small achievement will build momentum, motivating you to keep pushing forward.

As you work towards your goals, remember that flexibility is essential. Life is unpredictable, and circumstances can change, impacting your ability to follow through with your original plans. Regularly reviewing and adjusting your goals ensures that they remain relevant and feasible, promoting ongoing growth and adaptability. Here's how you can stay adaptive:

- Periodically evaluate your progress and setbacks.

- Ask yourself if your goals still align with your current values and priorities.

- Make necessary adjustments to your actions or timelines based on new insights or changes in circumstances.

- Embrace setbacks as learning opportunities rather than failures.

This willingness to adapt can turn obstacles into stepping stones, providing valuable lessons that propel you forward.

It's also crucial not to overlook the importance of celebrating your achievements, no matter how small they may seem. Acknowledging and celebrating your successes reinforces positive habits and boosts self-confidence. This celebration doesn't have to be grand; even simple acts like treating yourself to something you enjoy or sharing your accomplishments with loved ones can make a significant difference. Here's how you can effectively celebrate your progress:

- Recognize and document every small victory along the way.

- Share your achievements with friends or family to gain support and encouragement.

- Reward yourself with something meaningful, whether it's a relaxing day off or a favorite treat.

- Reflect on how far you've come and use that reflection as motivation for future goals.

By consistently recognizing your efforts and celebrating your milestones, you cultivate a sense of accomplishment that drives further success.

Setting meaningful goals provides direction and motivation for personal development. It gives you a roadmap to navigate the journey of personal growth, helping you stay focused and resilient amid life's challenges. This process of goal-setting, breaking down tasks, staying adaptable, and celebrating achievements fosters a cycle of continuous improvement and fulfillment.

So, as you embark on this journey of personal growth, remember that the path is uniquely yours. What works for someone else might not work for you, and that's perfectly okay. Your goals should reflect your individuality, your values, and your aspirations. Embrace change as an opportunity for transformation, and don't be afraid to adjust your course as you gather new experiences and insights.

In conclusion, setting meaningful goals anchored in your values is essential for personal development. By breaking these goals down into manageable steps, regularly reviewing and adjusting your approach, and celebrating your achievements, you pave the way for sustained growth and fulfillment. Remember, the journey is just as important as the destination. Stay curious, stay motivated, and allow change to be the catalyst that leads you towards a more fulfilling life.

Importance of Self-Awareness

Self-reflection enhances self-awareness and facilitates personal growth and emotional intelligence. Many of us are so caught up in our daily routines that we forget the importance of pausing and contemplating our actions, thoughts, and emotions. Taking just a few minutes out of each day to reflect can reveal patterns and habits we didn't even know existed. When we take the time to look inward, we begin to see ourselves more clearly, which can lead to significant personal growth.

Here is what you can do in order to achieve this goal:

- Set aside a few quiet moments each day to sit with your thoughts.

- Keep a journal where you can jot down your reflections, feelings, and insights.

- Ask yourself open-ended questions like "Why did I react that way?" or "What can I learn from this experience?"

Reflecting on these questions helps to enhance emotional intelligence by allowing us to manage our own emotions better and understand those of others. Emotional intelligence is key to navigating social complexities, nurturing relationships, and making informed decisions. By understanding our emotions, we also become more adept at regulating them, which can reduce stress and improve overall mental health.

Seeking feedback from others helps in gaining different perspectives and insights for self-improvement. Sometimes, our self-perception can be limited or biased. We might be blind to certain behaviors or tendencies that others find noticeable. This is why seeking feedback from trusted friends, family members, or colleagues can be invaluable. They can provide insights and viewpoints that we might miss on our own.

Here are some ways to seek and use feedback effectively:

- Approach people you trust and who you know will be honest with you.

- Be specific about what you want feedback on. If it's related to work, ask about your performance on a project or how you handle teamwork. If it's personal, inquire about your communication or behavior in various situations.

- Listen actively and without defense. Even if the feedback is hard to hear, try to understand it rather than immediately dismissing it.

Utilizing feedback constructively can lead to significant improvements in personal and professional areas of life. It allows us to see our blind spots and make adjustments that can enhance our effectiveness and relationships.

Embracing lifelong learning fosters personal development and keeps the mind open to new possibilities. The world is constantly changing, and clinging to outdated knowledge or beliefs can hinder our growth. Lifelong learning is about more than just picking up new skills; it's about maintaining a curious and open mindset throughout life. Whether it's reading books, taking courses, or simply exploring new hobbies, continuous learning keeps our minds engaged and versatile.

You can incorporate lifelong learning into your life by:

- Setting learning goals for yourself, such as mastering a new language, picking up a musical instrument, or diving into a subject you've always been curious about.

- Finding resources that resonate with you, whether they are books, podcasts, online courses, or even community workshops.

- Surrounding yourself with other learners who encourage and inspire you.

By committing to lifelong learning, we enrich our lives with new experiences and knowledge, keeping our minds sharp and our perspectives fresh. This ongoing process empowers us to adapt to changes more effectively and seize opportunities that come our way.

Practicing mindfulness can help individuals stay present and connected to their thoughts and emotions. In today's fast-paced world, it's easy to get lost in the past or worry incessantly about the future. Mindfulness teaches us to anchor ourselves in the present moment, creating a deep connection to our current thoughts, emotions, and surroundings.

To practice mindfulness, consider the following steps:

- Start with short periods of mindfulness meditation. Find a quiet spot, close your eyes, and focus on your breath. Notice how it feels as you inhale and exhale.

- During daily activities, such as eating or walking, pay close attention to the sensations, sounds, and smells around you. Engage fully with the present moment.

- Use mindfulness apps or guided meditations to help structure your practice and keep you consistent.

Mindfulness not only reduces stress but also enhances self-awareness by helping us recognize automatic thought patterns and emotional reactions. Over time, this practice can lead to a calmer, more balanced state of mind, aiding in better decision-making and emotional regulation.

In conclusion, self-awareness and continuous learning are crucial for personal growth and adaptability. Engaging in self-reflection, seeking feedback, embracing lifelong learning, and practicing mindfulness all contribute to a deepened understanding of ourselves and our surroundings.

These practices enable us to navigate life's challenges more effectively, fostering resilience and personal fulfillment.

When we commit to knowing ourselves better and staying open to new learning experiences, we lay a strong foundation for growth and transformation. These efforts are not just about improving individual aspects of our lives, but about creating enduring change that leads to a more fulfilling and purpose-driven existence.

Remember, the journey of personal growth is ongoing. Each step taken towards greater self-awareness and continual learning brings us closer to becoming the best versions of ourselves. So, take a breath, reflect, seek new insights, and embrace the endless possibilities that lie ahead. Your transformative journey has already begun.

Embracing Challenges

Imagine arriving at a crossroads in life where the very challenges you face become gateways to growth and self-improvement. It is often our perception that turns these moments of adversity into opportunities. By viewing challenges as learning experiences, we can begin to reframe them as a chance for personal development.

Consider the first time you rode a bicycle. Initially, it was intimidating, maybe even a bit terrifying. There were possibly tumbles, scrapes, and perhaps some frustration. But each fall taught you something new – balance, coordination, perseverance. Over time, with each attempt, you grew more confident. This example underscores how life's hurdles can serve as lessons rather than setbacks.

Reframing challenges this way involves an active shift in mindset. Here is what you can do in order to achieve this:

- Start by identifying the challenge at hand and acknowledging your feelings about it. It's okay to feel overwhelmed.

- Break down the challenge into smaller, manageable tasks. This approach can make even the most daunting obstacles seem conquerable.

- Look for the silver lining. Ask yourself, "What can I learn from this?" or "How can this situation help me grow?"

Developing resilience through overcoming challenges builds strength and perseverance. Resilience is not just about bouncing back; it's about growing stronger with each setback. Think of a tree weathering a storm. The winds may bend and stress its branches, yet once the storm passes, the tree stands firm, roots dug deeper into the soil.

Every time life throws a curveball, and you overcome it, you add a layer of fortitude to your character. The process of tackling difficulties head-on teaches you tenacity. You learn that while the journey might be arduous, the rewards are profoundly fulfilling. Those battle scars you carry are marks of honor, each one telling a story of survival and growth.

Here's how to build resilience:

- Practice self-compassion. Acknowledge that it's okay to struggle and remind yourself that growth often comes from discomfort.

- Stay connected with supportive friends, family, or communities. Sharing your journey can provide encouragement and different perspectives.

- Focus on what you can control. Sometimes, the uncontrollable aspects of a situation can overwhelm us. Zeroing in on actionable steps can restore a sense of agency and calm.

Seeking out new challenges is another strategy that can help individuals expand their comfort zones and develop new skills. Stepping out of familiar territory can be unnerving, but it's also where significant growth begins. Attempting something novel, like learning a new language or taking up a new hobby, can open doors to talents and strengths you never knew existed.

Embrace the unknown, for it's the place where possibility flourishes. Each new endeavor brings with it a set of lessons that broaden your skillset and enrich your life experience. It's like planting seeds in a garden; every new challenge you take on is a seed that, nurtured with effort and patience, will bloom into rewarding achievements.

To enthusiastically seek out challenges, try the following:

- Set small, attainable goals that push you slightly beyond your current abilities. These incremental steps can make larger challenges feel more approachable.

- Embrace a curious mindset. Whether you're trying something entirely new or revisiting old skills, staying curious can keep the experience enjoyable and engaging.

- Reflect on past successes. Remembering the times you've succeeded despite initial doubts can motivate you to pursue new ventures with confidence.

Finally, embracing failures as part of the learning process encourages a resilience and growth mindset. Failure is often misunderstood as a dead-end when, in reality, it's a pit stop on the road to success. Every misstep reveals valuable information about what doesn't work, steering you closer to strategies that do.

Think of figures like Thomas Edison, who viewed his many unsuccessful attempts at inventing the light bulb as steps towards eventual success. Rather than giving up, he saw each failure as a necessary discovery process. Adopting this perspective allows you to approach challenges without fear of failure obstructing your path.

To embrace failure constructively, consider these approaches:

- Shift your perspective on failure. Instead of seeing it as an endpoint, view it as feedback.

- Analyze what went wrong. Breaking down the failure to understand its components can offer insights for future attempts.

- Celebrate your efforts. Acknowledge the courage it takes to try, regardless of the outcome. This positive reinforcement can bolster your willingness to tackle new challenges.

Ultimately, the key takeaway here is that embracing challenges with a positive attitude can lead to profound personal growth and self-improvement. It's not the absence of struggle that defines us, but how we choose to confront and learn from it. Life's tribulations, when perceived through the lens of opportunity, can transform into powerful catalysts for growth.

By consistently viewing challenges as potential learning experiences, developing resilience, seeking out new endeavors, and embracing failure, you cultivate an environment in which you can thrive. Each step forward, no matter how small, is progress towards a more resilient, capable, and fulfilled version of yourself.

So next time life presents a challenge, inhale deeply, remember the countless ways you've grown from past adversities, and step forward with renewed purpose. Your future self is waiting, stronger and wiser, shaped beautifully by every bump and bruise along the way.

The Power of Embracing Change

In reflecting on the journey through life's transitions, we've explored the notion that accepting change is key to building resilience and adaptability. Life moves much like a river—sometimes swift and unpredictable, other times calm and reflective. Embracing this constant flux allows us to develop strength and flexibility, making even the most daunting changes feel more manageable.

We started by emphasizing that developing flexible thinking is essential in navigating life's twists and turns. Being open to different solutions and perspectives can transform challenges into opportunities for growth. By questioning assumptions, practicing mindfulness, and engaging in diverse activities, we expand our mental toolkit, effectively preparing ourselves for whatever comes our way.

Embracing uncertainty was another significant point. While stepping into the unknown can be intimidating, it also opens doors to profound personal growth and discovery. Reflecting on past experiences where uncertainty led to positive outcomes reveals its hidden potential for cultivating resilience and uncovering new paths.

Also highlighted was the importance of seeking support during transitions. Human connection is foundational to our well-being, and reaching out to friends, family, or professionals can provide comfort and guidance. Sharing our struggles and leaning on others not only fosters emotional support but also offers fresh insights and perspectives that help illuminate our way forward.

Ultimately, embracing change is about recognizing it as a natural—and beneficial—part of life's journey. Change doesn't have to be feared; it can be welcomed as a catalyst for self-discovery and improvement. Whether it's through developing flexible thinking, embracing uncertainty, or seeking support, each step taken towards embracing change brings us closer to a more fulfilling and resilient life.

As you continue on your path, remember that every transition carries the potential for transformation. View each change as a guiding force, urging you towards experiences that enrich your life with wisdom, resilience, and joy. Let this perspective guide you as you welcome the changes life brings, knowing that they hold the promise of growth and fulfillment. Above all, cherish the journey with its highs and lows, for it shapes you into the person you are meant to become. Indeed, your transformative journey has already begun, with every step bringing you closer to the best version of yourself.

Chapter 8: Sustaining Mental Wellness Long-Term

Sustaining Mental Wellness Long-T

I magine waking up each day with a sense of calm, purpose, and resilience. The journey to this state of mental well-being is not a straight path but a continuously evolving process that requires dedication, self-awareness, and the right strategies. For many, achieving sustained mental wellness can feel like an elusive goal overshadowed by stress, life challenges, and lingering trauma. However, with the right tools and habits in place, you can transform this aspiration into a lasting reality.

For numerous individuals, initial strides towards mental health improvement often falter without consistent practices and support systems. Consider the common scenario of adopting a new fitness routine – initial enthusiasm soon wanes if not integrated into daily life. Similarly, sporadic acts of self-care cannot anchor long-term mental stability. The absence of regularity in activities such as exercise, balanced nutrition, and meaningful social interactions leaves many struggling to maintain their progress. Moreover, the lack of a strong support network can compound feelings of isolation and helplessness, further derailing efforts towards sustained mental wellness.

In this chapter, we will explore practical strategies to nurture and sustain your mental wellness over time. You will learn how consistency in self-care practices, such as regular physical activity and mindful eating, can significantly boost your mental state. We'll delve into the importance of building and maintaining a robust support network, which can provide much-needed emotional backing during tough times. Furthermore, we will discuss engaging in activities that bring joy and fulfillment, alongside techniques for regularly assessing your mental health to stay proactive in your wellness journey. These combined approaches aim to arm you with a comprehensive toolkit to foster enduring mental health and personal growth.

Strategies for Maintaining Mental Health Progress Over Time

Maintaining mental wellness is an ongoing process, pivoting around a few core strategies. These strategies not only facilitate initial mental health improvements but also ensure that progress continues over time.

Consistency in self-care practices is indispensable for long-term mental well-being. Establishing and maintaining regular habits like exercise and healthy eating can make a substantial difference. How you treat your body directly impacts how you feel mentally. For those looking to cement these habits into their routines, here are some steps to consider:

- Start by integrating short periods of physical activity into your daily schedule, such as a brisk walk or a simple stretching routine.

- Gradually increase the intensity and duration of your exercises once you get accustomed to the basic routine.

- Ensure your diet is balanced with nutrients that boost brain function; include foods rich in omega-3 fatty acids, antioxidants, and vitamins.

- Plan your meals ahead to avoid unhealthy last-minute food choices, keeping a variety of healthy snacks accessible.

- Stay hydrated throughout the day, mindful of how different beverages affect your mood and energy levels.

Next, building a strong support network is crucial for sustaining mental wellness over time. Human connections play an undeniable role in our psychological health. It's not merely about having people around but fostering meaningful relationships where you feel valued and understood. To nurture such connections, you might follow these guidelines:

- Reach out to friends or family members regularly, even if it's just a quick check-in message or phone call.

- Participate in group activities that interest you, whether it's a book club, a sports league, or volunteer work.

- Be open and vulnerable in conversations, sharing your feelings honestly and listening empathetically to others.

- Offer support to others when they need it; giving support can also positively impact your own mental health.

- Don't hesitate to seek professional help if personal connections aren't sufficient; therapists and counselors can provide structured support and guidance (National Institutes of Health (NIH), 2017).

Engaging in activities that bring joy and fulfillment is another significant element in the equation. When you immerse yourself in pursuits that you love, it naturally fosters a positive mental outlook. Whether it's painting, gardening, playing an instrument, or hiking – the key lies in finding what resonates with you and making it a regular part of your life. What brings joy to one person might not do the same for another, so it's essential to explore different activities and identify those that genuinely make you feel uplifted.

Finally, regularly assessing your mental health status ensures you stay on track and address issues before they escalate. Self-awareness is a powerful tool in managing mental wellness. By routinely checking in with yourself and evaluating how you're doing, you become more adept at recognizing when things might be veering off course. Here's what you can do to keep tabs on your mental health:

- Maintain a journal where you record your thoughts, feelings, and experiences on a daily or weekly basis. This helps you track patterns and triggers.

- Use digital tools and apps designed for mental health tracking; they can offer insights and reminders for self-care.

- Schedule periodic check-ins with a mental health professional, even when you're feeling fine. Regular consultations can prevent minor issues from becoming major problems (kconvery, 2021).

- Develop a set of personal indicators that signal when you might need extra support, such as changes in sleep patterns, appetite fluctuations, or increased irritability.

- Create a contingency plan that includes steps to take and resources to contact if you notice a decline in your mental health.

By combining consistency in self-care practices, nurturing supportive relationships, engaging in joyful activities, and regularly assessing your mental health, you create a sustainable approach to mental wellness. Remember, this journey is unique to everyone, and there's no one-size-fits-all solution. But by embracing these strategies, you lay a solid foundation for enduring mental health and well-being.

The Role of Self-Monitoring and Reflection in Personal Growth

Developing a sustainable approach to mental wellness is essential for continued growth and well-being. Let's delve into the role of self-monitoring and reflection in personal growth, and how it can be a cornerstone for anyone looking to enhance their mental health.

Regular self-assessment and reflection allow individuals to track their progress and identify areas for improvement on their mental wellness journey. Self-awareness is the first step to improvement, and it's often said that "you can't change what you don't acknowledge." Setting aside regular time to assess your mental state can offer invaluable insights. This practice can reveal patterns in your behavior and thoughts that either help or hinder your well-being.

Here is what you can do:

- Start by setting a specific time each week for self-assessment. This could be at the end of each day or weekly on Sunday evening.

- Use tools like mood trackers, which are available as apps, or simply maintain a journal where you jot down your feelings and significant events of the day.

By honestly assessing your mental state regularly, you create a log of your emotions and the factors influencing them. This pattern recognition is crucial (Williams, n.d.).

Next, setting aside time for introspection and journaling can aid in processing emotions and thoughts, leading to personal growth. Journaling acts as a mirror to your inner world. It helps make sense of complex emotions, digests life experiences, and sometimes reveals underlying issues you weren't fully conscious of. When you write things down, you're not just recording; you're also clarifying.

Here is what you can do:

- Dedicate a few minutes daily to free-write whatever comes to mind—no censorship.

- Reflect on questions like: What made me feel happy today? What was a challenge? How did I handle it?

- Review your journal entries periodically to observe growth or recurring themes that need addressing.

This habit of introspective writing not only aids emotional release but also empowers you to become proactive in managing your mental health (Leschber, 2023).

Developing mindfulness practices can increase self-awareness and help in recognizing triggers that may impact mental well-being. Mindfulness is paying attention to the present moment without judgment. It's about being aware of your thoughts, feelings, and sensations as they happen. This heightened awareness can help you notice early signs of stress or anxiety before they grow overwhelming.

Here is what you can do:

- Practice deep breathing exercises. Simple techniques such as inhaling slowly for four counts, holding for four counts, and exhaling for four counts can calm your mind.

- Engage in short daily meditation sessions. Apps like Headspace or Calm can guide you through this process.

- Be mindful during everyday activities. Whether eating, walking, or even washing dishes, pay full attention to the task at hand.

These mindfulness practices help in staying grounded, reducing the mental clutter, and recognizing triggers for stress, making it easier to address them proactively (Harvard Business Review, 2022).

Embracing a growth mindset and viewing challenges as opportunities for learning foster continuous personal development. A growth mindset is the belief that talents can be developed through hard work, good strategies, and input from others. This contrasts with a fixed mindset, where people believe their qualities are static and unchangeable. Adopting a growth mindset means seeing challenges and failures not as indicators of one's limitations but as valuable learning experiences.

Consider a scenario where you face a setback at work. Instead of berating yourself for the mistake, you could ask reflective questions like: What went wrong? What can I learn from this experience? How can I improve moving forward? This shift in perception can transform challenges into stepping stones for betterment.

A part of fostering a growth mindset also involves celebrating small wins along the journey. Small accomplishments build confidence and keep you motivated to tackle bigger goals. After all, change doesn't always have to be monumental; often, it's the accumulation of small, consistent changes that lead to significant transformation.

By integrating these self-monitoring and reflective practices into your routine, you not only enhance your mental wellness but also build resilience and capacity for continuous personal growth. Remember, though, this is not an overnight transformation. It's a gradual, ongoing process that demands patience and persistence. The key is to remain committed to these practices and compassionate towards yourself throughout the journey.

As you continue this path to mental wellness, you'll find that self-assessment, journaling, mindfulness, and a growth mindset serve as powerful tools in your arsenal. They collectively empower you to navigate life's ups and downs with greater ease and grace, ensuring not just survival but thriving in every aspect of your life.

Importance of Seeking Ongoing Support and Professional Guidance

Developing a sustainable approach to mental wellness is essential for continued growth and well-being. One pivotal aspect of this journey involves seeking ongoing support and professional guidance. This isn't just a luxury; it's a necessity for fostering resilience and ensuring that you have the tools to navigate life's inevitable challenges.

Regular therapy sessions or counseling can provide valuable insights and coping strategies to maintain mental wellness. Therapy offers a safe space where you can explore your thoughts, feelings, and behaviors with the guidance of a trained professional. Engaging in regular therapy or counseling sessions helps create a structured environment for personal growth. It provides a foundation upon which you can build healthier patterns of thinking and behaving.

Here is what you can do in order to achieve the goal:

- Find a licensed therapist whose expertise aligns with your needs. You can look for recommendations from friends, family, or online directories.

- Prepare for your sessions by reflecting on any specific issues or topics you'd like to address.

- Be open and honest during your sessions. The more you share, the more your therapist can help.

- Practice the techniques and strategies discussed during sessions in your daily life. Consistency is key.

- Schedule regular follow-ups to monitor progress and adjust treatment plans as needed.

Joining support groups or community programs can offer a sense of belonging and understanding during challenging times. These groups are often comprised of individuals who share similar experiences and struggles, creating an environment of empathy and mutual support. Whether it's a local group meeting in person or an online community, these connections can be incredibly comforting and validating.

Here is what you can do in order to achieve the goal:

- Look for support groups that focus on your specific concerns. This could range from anxiety and depression to substance use or trauma recovery.

- Attend a few different groups to find one that feels like the right fit. Each group has its own dynamic, and it's important to feel comfortable.

- Participate actively but at your own pace. Share when you're ready and listen to others. This balance can enhance both your experience and the support you provide to others.

- Leverage the shared resources and activities offered by the group. These might include workshops, mindfulness sessions, or social gatherings.

- Build relationships within the group. Having trusted people to turn to outside of scheduled meetings extends the support network into everyday life.

Consulting with mental health professionals allows for tailored treatment plans and interventions to address specific mental health needs. Each individual's mental health journey is unique, requiring solutions that are specifically designed to address their circumstances. Mental health professionals, such as psychiatrists, psychologists, and clinical social workers, possess the expertise to diagnose conditions accurately and recommend appropriate treatments, whether that includes medication, cognitive-behavioral strategies, or other therapeutic approaches.

Here is what you can do in order to achieve the goal:

- Start with a general practitioner or psychologist to assess your overall mental health and get referrals if needed.

- Ensure you're comfortable with the professional you choose. A good rapport enhances the effectiveness of the treatment.

- Discuss all symptoms openly and ask questions about potential diagnoses and treatment options.

- Follow through with prescribed treatment plans, including attending appointments regularly and taking medications as directed.

- Keep track of changes in symptoms and communicate these to your healthcare provider to fine-tune your treatment plan.

Educating oneself about mental health resources and staying informed on available support systems enhances long-term mental well-being. Knowledge empowers you to make informed decisions regarding your health and to advocate for yourself effectively.

There are numerous resources available, ranging from books and scholarly articles to webinars and podcasts that discuss various aspects of mental health.

Staying informed also means being aware of the latest advancements in mental health care and understanding your rights as a patient. For instance, many workplaces are now recognizing the importance of mental health and are incorporating supportive measures (Why mental health needs to be a top priority in the workplace, n.d.). Knowing about these organizational shifts can help you seek out environments that prioritize mental wellness.

Incorporating these strategies requires commitment, but the benefits are profound. A sustainable approach to mental wellness not only addresses immediate concerns but also fosters resilience, allowing you to thrive in the face of life's challenges. By integrating regular therapy, participating in support groups, consulting professionals, and staying educated, you build a robust framework that supports mental well-being throughout your life.

This multifaceted approach aligns with empirical evidence showing the positive impacts of comprehensive mental health strategies. For instance, having a strong support system is linked to higher levels of well-being and better coping skills (NCSP, 2020). These components work synergistically to provide a solid foundation for mental health, enhancing not only individual wellness but contributing to healthier communities overall. As we each take steps toward maintaining our mental health, we contribute to breaking down the stigma surrounding mental health issues, paving the way for a more compassionate and understanding society.

Creating a Personalized Wellness Plan for Long-Term Mental Well-Being

Developing a sustainable approach to mental wellness is essential for continued growth and well-being. It's not just about addressing crises as they arise, but about building a foundation that supports you through all of life's ups and downs. Creating a personalized wellness plan is key to achieving long-term mental health.

Setting clear and achievable mental health goals helps in staying motivated and focused on self-improvement.

Think of mental health goals like a roadmap guiding you towards happiness and stability. Without these goals, it can be easy to feel lost or overwhelmed. Setting goals provides direction and a sense of purpose. However, goals need to be realistic and tailored to your unique situation.

Here is what you can do in order to achieve this:

- Start by identifying the areas of your life where you feel changes could improve your mental health. Is it reducing anxiety, improving mood, or increasing social connections?

- Break down these broad goals into smaller, specific, and actionable steps. If you're looking to reduce anxiety, a goal might be to practice meditation for ten minutes every morning.

- Make sure your goals are measurable. Instead of saying, "I want to feel less anxious," aim for something like, "I will practice mindfulness meditation for ten minutes daily."

- Track your progress regularly. Write down your achievements and setbacks to see patterns and modify your actions as needed.

- Celebrate small victories. Recognize and reward yourself for accomplishing even minor steps toward your bigger goals.

Incorporating a variety of self-care practices into daily routines ensures holistic well-being and balanced mental health.

Self-care isn't just a trendy buzzword; it's a crucial element of maintaining mental health. A variety of activities nurture different aspects of well-being, including physical, emotional, and social dimensions.

Daily routines should embed these diverse practices to create a resilient mental health buffer.

Here is what you can do to integrate self-care into your routine:

- Start with simple activities. Incorporate basic self-care habits like drinking enough water, getting adequate sleep, and eating nutritious meals.

- Engage in enjoyable activities. Whether it's a hobby like painting or a relaxing bath, ensure you're doing things that bring joy and relaxation.

- Foster social connections. Schedule regular meet-ups with friends or family. Even a weekly phone call can significantly boost your mental health.

- Practice mindfulness. Set aside time each day for meditation, breathing exercises, or simply sitting quietly and reflecting.

- Balance work and rest. Allocate time for productivity but equally prioritize breaks and downtime to recharge.

Developing coping strategies for managing stress and adversity equips individuals with tools to navigate challenges in the long run.

Stress and adversity are inevitable. What differentiates those who cope well from those who struggle often boils down to their strategies for managing these pressures. Effective coping mechanisms provide you with resilience during tough times and help maintain mental equilibrium.

Here is what you can do to develop coping strategies:

- Identify your stress triggers. Understanding what induces stress can help you prepare and manage your reactions better.

- Develop a toolbox of coping skills. This could include deep-breathing exercises, journaling feelings, or taking short walks to clear your mind.

- Learn problem-solving techniques. When faced with challenging situations, break them down into manageable parts and address them one step at a time.

- Reach out for support. Do not hesitate to contact friends, family, or professionals when things get overwhelming. Sometimes, talking about your stressors can lighten the load.

- Practice relaxation techniques. Incorporate activities like yoga, progressive muscle relaxation, or tai chi into your routine to facilitate calmness.

Regularly reviewing and adjusting the wellness plan based on individual needs and experiences promotes adaptability and growth in the journey towards sustained mental wellness.

A wellness plan isn't a set-it-and-forget-it kind of deal. Life changes, and so do our needs and circumstances. Regular reviews and adjustments ensure that the wellness plan remains relevant and effective over time.

Here is what you can do to keep your wellness plan updated:

- Set regular check-in appointments with yourself. Every month or quarter, take dedicated time to review your goals and self-care practices.

- Reflect on what's working and what's not. Be honest about the strategies that help and those that don't.

- Adapt your plan to current circumstances. Maybe a particular coping strategy isn't as effective anymore? That's okay. Adjust your approach and try new techniques.

- Seek feedback from trusted sources. Friends, family, or mental health professionals can offer valuable insights into areas you might overlook.

- Stay flexible. Understand that it's normal for your mental health needs to evolve. An adaptable mindset makes it easier to tweak your wellness plan as you grow and change.

Creating a personalized wellness plan is not just a reactive measure but a proactive investment in long-term mental health. By setting clear goals, integrating self-care practices, developing coping strategies, and continually reviewing and adjusting your plan, you carve a path towards enduring well-being. Remember, it's a process requiring patience and perseverance, but the result—an enriched, balanced life—is worth every effort.

References:

- Developing a Wellness Toolbox for Your Mental Health | HPU Online, n.d.

- Learn about the components of a mental health wellness plan and how to create a mental health wellness plan tailored for you on HealthyPlace., n.d.

- The Jed Foundation, 2024

Embracing Sustainable Mental Wellness Practices

In this chapter, we've delved into the multifaceted approach necessary for maintaining long-term mental wellness. We explored vital strategies like consistency in self-care, fostering supportive relationships, engaging in joyful activities, and regular mental health assessments. These foundations are crucial for ensuring that your journey towards mental wellness is sustainable and effective.

Reflecting on our discussion, it's clear that developing a sustainable approach to mental wellness requires commitment and mindfulness. Self-monitoring and reflection play pivotal roles in personal growth. Regular self-assessment allows you to track progress, recognize areas needing improvement, and understand patterns in your behavior and thoughts. This self-awareness is not just about identifying problems; it's about celebrating small victories and continually evolving.

Our position remains firm: building these habits is an ongoing process, unique to each individual, but universally beneficial. However, it's essential to acknowledge that some readers might feel overwhelmed when starting or maintaining these practices. You may encounter challenges in integrating new habits or sustaining motivation over the long haul. It's important to remain patient with yourself and seek support when needed.

The broader implications of neglecting mental wellness can be profound. Mental health issues left unaddressed can impact various aspects of life, from personal relationships to professional performance. On a wider scale, societies benefit immensely when individuals prioritize their mental health, leading to more compassionate, resilient communities.

As you continue your journey, remember that mental wellness is not a destination but a continuous path of growth. Embrace the strategies that resonate with you, be open to adaptations, and seek support along the way. Each step taken towards mindful self-care and emotional well-being contributes significantly to your overall happiness and resilience. Keep moving forward, knowing that every effort made today lays the groundwork for a healthier, more balanced tomorrow.

References

Williams, S. (n.d.). *Self-awareness* . Retrieved from https://f5webserv.wright.edu/~scott.williams/ LeaderLetter/selfawareness.htm

Harvard Business Review. (2022). *Don't underestimate the power of self-reflection* . Retrieved from https://hbr.org/2022/03/dont-underestimate-the-power-of-self-reflection

Hawai'i Pacific University. (n.d.). *Developing a Wellness Toolbox for Your Mental Health* . Retrieved from https://online.hpu.edu/blog/wellness-toolbox

Søvold, L. E., Naslund, J. A., Kousoulis, A. A., Saxena, S., Qoronfleh, M. W., Grobler, C., & Münter, L. (2021). *Prioritizing the mental health and well-being of healthcare workers: An urgent global public health priority* . *Frontiers in Public Health* , 9, Article 679397. https://doi.org/10.3389/fpubh.2021.679397

JED Foundation. (2024). *Create a Plan to Take Care of Your Mental Health* . *The Jed Foundation* . Retrieved from https://jedfoundation.org/resource/ create-a-plan-to-take-care-of-your-mental-health/

American Psychological Association. (2022). *U.S. Surgeon General cites APA research in new guidance around strengthening workplace well-being* . Retrieved from https://www.apa.org/news/apa/ 2022/surgeon-general-workplace-well-being

HealthyPlace. (n.d.). *How to develop a mental health wellness plan* . Retrieved from http://mylgc.org/ how-to-develop-a-mental-health-wellness-plan.html

National Institute of Mental Health (NIMH). *Caring for Your Mental Health* . Retrieved from https:// www.nimh.nih.gov/health/topics/caring-for-your- mental-health

National Institutes of Health (NIH). (2017). *Emotional Wellness Toolkit* . Retrieved from https://

www.nih.gov/health-information/emotional-wellness-toolkit

Leschber, C. (2023). *The art of self-reflection: Unlocking personal growth and fulfillment* . *BlogPosting* . Retrieved from https://www.romans-12two.org/the-art-of-self-reflection-unlocking-personal-growth-and-fulfillment

Hood, J. (2020). *The benefits and importance of a support system* . *Highland Springs Clinic* . Retrieved from https://highlandspringsclinic.org/the-benefits-and-importance-of-a-support-system/

Harvard Pilgrim Health Care. (2021). *How to find success in your mental health journey* . Harvard Pilgrim Health Care - HaPi Guide. Retrieved from https://www.harvardpilgrim.org/hapiguide/how-to-find-success-in-your-mental-health-journey/